MAIMONIDES

A Guide for Today's Perplexed

MAIMONIDES

A Guide for Today's Perplexed

KENNETH SEESKIN

Behrman House, Inc.

Library of Congress Cataloging-in-Publication Data

Seeskin, Kenneth, 1947–
    Maimonides : a guide for today's perplexed /
Kenneth Seeskin.
        p.   cm.
    Includes bibliographical references.
    ISBN 0-87441-509-8
    1. Maimonides, Moses, 1135-1204. Dalàlat
al-hà'irìn. 2. Judaism—Doctrines. 3. Philosophy,
Jewish. 4. Philosophy, Medieval.
    I. Title.
BM545.D35S42   1991   90–22162
181'.06—dc20   CIP

Published by   **Behrman House, Inc.**

ISBN 10: 0-87441-509-8
ISBN 13: 978-0-87441-509-4

Design by Seymour Rossel
Typesetting by RCC, Inc.

CONTENTS

To Alexander

My buddy, now and always

Acknowledgments

I devised the plan for this book in the winter of 1988 while teaching classes on Maimonides in two Chicago-area synagogues: North Suburban Synagogue Beth El and my own Ezra-Habonim. I wish to thank both institutions for inviting me to lecture and providing a stimulating forum in which to try out new material. I also wish to thank all those who read and commented on earlier versions of the manuscript: Joseph Edelheit, James M. Edie, Julie P. Gordon, Menachem Kellner, Manfred Vogel, and the late Steven S. Schwarzschild. Finally, I wish to thank Abraham Rothberg for valuable editorial assistance.

Throughout this study, I have used the Pines translation of *The Guide of the Perplexed*, published by The University of Chicago Press. Other editions and anthologies are mentioned in the Appendix. For the sake of uniformity, I have taken all biblical references from the Jewish Publication Society's edition of the Holy Scriptures.

MAIMONIDES

A Guide for Today's Perplexed

INTRODUCTION

Moses son of Maimon (known to English-speaking audiences as Maimonides, and to Hebrew-speaking ones as Ram-Bam) was born in Cordova, in southern Spain, in 1135. Shortly after the age of 13, he was forced to flee because the town was captured by an extremist Muslim sect, the Almohads. After journeying through North Africa, and eventually to the Holy Land, he settled in the outskirts of Cairo, where he did the majority of his scholarly and scientific work. He died in 1204.

Maimonides' learning was legendary. There was scarcely a subject, Jewish or secular, in which he did not make an original contribution. Completely familiar with biblical and rabbinic literature, his 14-volume study of Jewish law, the *Mishneh Torah,* is perhaps the greatest such compilation ever attempted. Maimonides finds an important philosophic or scientific principle behind every Jewish custom, practice, or prohibition; every law is a way of enhancing spiritual development, a process which reaches its culmination in the rational love of God. But his contributions do not end there. He was also deeply versed in philosophic literature, particularly the neo-Aristotelian currents in Jewish and Islamic thought. His writings indicate that he had a thorough knowledge of the physics, astronomy, mathematics, and logic of his time. He was a practicing physician whose reputation was known in faraway lands. His popular works show that, in addition to writing treatises on science and philosophy, he took an active part in the religious and political controversies of his day. Author, teacher, court physician, director of a public clinic, and spiritual leader of the Jewish community in Cairo, he was both a theoretician and a man of action.

Maimonides' philosophic reputation rests on his masterpiece, *The Guide of the Perplexed*, published in Arabic in 1190 and quickly translated into Hebrew. Unfortunately, it is difficult for the average person living in the twentieth century to read *The Guide* with any degree of comprehension. First, there is the difficulty of its length: three volumes and a total of 178 chapters. The second difficulty is the learning the author presupposes. Maimonides did not intend for the book to be read by a general audience. He assumes his readers are familiar with the sacred literature of Judaism, the classics of Greek philosophy, and later medieval commentaries. The last difficulty is that the book was written during the twelfth century, and since then our view of the world has undergone numerous changes. The Aristotelian vocabulary used by Maimonides and his contemporaries fell into disrepute with the rise of modern science. The notion that heavenly bodies are composed of a different matter than earthly bodies and therefore behave according to different laws is no longer accepted. As a result, those of us who live in the twentieth century cannot help but find the world of *The Guide* somewhat foreign. According to Abraham J. Heschel, Maimonides' influence on people has been "indirect and altogether heterogeneous."

The present study attempts to rectify this situation, to make *The Guide* accessible to people with no formal training in philosophy. Although Maimonides had a number of philosophic predecessors, both Jewish and Islamic, he rarely discusses them in detail; his usual strategy is to present arguments as clearly as he can and evaluate them on their merits. For that reason, this volume does not probe very deeply into the works of other thinkers. Rather than present the history of an entire period, it attempts to analyze and evaluate the contributions of one of the period's leading figures, selecting a handful of representative themes to show how they form a coherent picture of Maimonides' thought.

Simplification runs the risk of distortion. In making Maimonides accessible to people with no training in philosophy, I cannot do justice to the richness and subtlety of his thought. But one also runs a risk in allowing the work of a great thinker to be ignored. Under the circumstances, the best strategy is to introduce Maimonides and hope that people will be encouraged to read his philosophy at a more advanced level.

CHAPTER ONE

WHY IS ANYONE PERPLEXED?

> *Behold, I have taught you statutes and ordinances, even as the Lord my God commanded me, that ye should do so in the midst of the land whither ye go in to possess it. Observe therefore and do them; for this is your wisdom and your understanding in the sight of the peoples, that, when they hear all these statutes, shall say: "Surely this great nation is a wise and understanding people."*
>
> Deuteronomy 4:5–6

WHY IS
ANYONE
PERPLEXED?

1. Does Monotheism
Mean Belief in One God?

Shema Yisrael Adonoi Eloheynu Adonoi Ehad. "Hear, O Israel:
the Lord Our God, the Lord is One." These words, repeated
twice a day, have been central to Jewish religious affirmation for centuries. Children learned them on their mothers'
knees; martyrs have gone to their deaths chanting them out
loud. But what do they mean? What does it mean to profess
monotheism?

The most obvious answer is that monotheism (mono +
theism) holds that there is only one God or supreme being,
not many. A pagan culture like ancient Greece's believed that
there were 12 deities on Mt. Olympus, but Judaism asserts
that the deity must be single. As obvious as this answer may
seem, it misses a critical point. In chapter six, we will consider
the question of idolatry from a contemporary perspective.
For the present, it is helpful to stay with a simple example.
Suppose someone living in ancient Greece had said that of
the 12 deities on Mt. Olympus, 11 of them are fakes; the only
true one is Athena, who lives in a palace on top of the
mountain and goes about in full battle attire. She eats nectar
and ambrosia, can cause natural phenomena like storms or
floods, but is herself subject to the impersonal decrees of fate.
Suppose, in addition, that this ancient Greek claimed to be a
monotheist. After all, according to this person's belief there
is only one god: Athena. It happens that she can be depicted

in a graven image, but she is the only god in the universe. It is clear that belief in the sole divinity of Athena would not be *monotheistic* as Judaism understands the term. What, then, is the difference between true monotheism—the kind Jews have been willing to die for—and the kind of paganism which recognizes a single deity? If believing in a single deity is not the distinguishing feature of monotheism, what is?

These are not easy problems to resolve. They force a Jew, or anyone else who adheres to a monotheistic religion, to raise what could be troubling issues. They challenge believers in monotheism to do philosophy. A typical response to this challenge is to ignore it. Critics point out that people have engaged in philosophic speculation for thousands of years and are still arguing about basic principles. Why complicate religious belief by introducing questions to which there may be no certain answer? Why not say the *Shema* at the required times and not concern oneself with philosophic refinements?

The answer is that if Jews have gone to their deaths affirming the *Shema*, surely monotheism is more than just a philosophic refinement. Unless Judaism has been wrong all these years, monotheism must be an essential truth—nay, the single most basic truth a person can learn. So in order to proclaim monotheism *and to know what one is proclaiming*, one must make an intellectual effort. It is not enough to speak the six words of the *Shema* as one might utter a magical incantation; one must think about God, unity, and the making of images in a systematic way.

Consider the Second Commandment: "Thou shalt not make unto thee a graven image, nor any manner of likeness, of any thing that is in heaven above, or that is in the earth beneath, or that is in the water under the earth: thou shalt not bow down unto them, nor serve them . . ." A person sins against this commandment by worshipping idols. Abraham ibn Ezra, a medieval Jewish philosopher, added that we must be careful not to sin against the Second Commandment *in thought*, by which he meant that a person who refrains from idol worship but envisions God in a material way is still committing a sin. The logic of his position is straightforward. It will not do to say that making images of God is a sin but that it is all right to conceive of God as if He *could* be imaged. A person who thinks of God as a man sitting on a throne is violating the Commandment by thinking of God as an ancient Greek would have thought of Athena: in anthropomorphic terms. There would then be little to distinguish Judaism from single-deity paganism.

It may be objected that Scripture is full of passages which imply that God does sit on a throne — that He walks, has a face, arms, changes physical location, and speaks in an audible voice. Moses refers to the throne of the Lord in Exodus 17:16. In Isaiah 6:1, the prophet maintains: "I beheld my Lord seated on a high and lofty throne; and the skirts of His robe filled the Temple." Genesis 6:9 says that Noah walked with God. Exodus 19 claims that God will come down in sight of the people and descend on Mt. Sinai. Isaiah 40:22 portrays God as sitting over the circle of the earth. Exodus 33:11 says that the Lord spoke to Moses "face to face." Repeatedly, Scripture says God brought Israel out of Egypt with a mighty hand and an outstretched arm.

Clearly something is out of joint. Judaism rejects the pagan worldview, and the practice of worshipping graven images — a common one in the ancient world — was prohibited categorically. If the full implications of this prohibition are understood, not only are images objectionable in fact, they are objectionable in the imagery one uses in one's own mind. If it is wrong to imagine God in a human shape in one context, it is equally wrong in the other. Yet the sacred literature of Judaism consistently uses anthropomorphic terms to characterize God. How can it be that the sacred writings appear to do what monotheism and the Second Commandment prohibit? Once again, we must raise philosophic questions. Read in a literal way, the sacred writings depict God as an ancient Greek would have depicted Athena. On the other hand, our own reason tells us that God cannot sit on a throne or occupy a physical location "above" the earth. The *Shema* tells us that God is somehow one, but it is not clear what that means.

This is the sort of perplexity which Maimonides strove to address. In a way, *The Guide of the Perplexed* is a simple

book: It is nothing but a discussion of monotheism and its
implications. It has two overriding assumptions:

(1)   The Torah and the sacred writings of Judaism are true;
(2)   The Torah and the sacred writings of Judaism do not
       ask us to accept anything reason shows to be
       impossible.

Putting these two assumptions together, we can see that
for Maimonides the Torah is an educational vehicle, a body
of wisdom. Reduced to simplest terms, the Torah asks one
thing: that we abandon idolatry and everything connected
with it. It commands us not to make images of God. It
prohibits sorcery, divination, and attempts to communicate
with the dead (Deuteronomy 18:10). It does not ask us to
accept mysteries or other seemingly irrational doctrines "on
faith." The life Torah sets before us is one in which the
absurdity of idolatry is so manifest that we are not even
tempted to embrace it. Such a life would require nothing less
than a moral and intellectual transformation. We have seen
that idolatry and monotheism are not easy to define, but why
should they be? Why should a truth as important as monotheism be as simple as the six words of the *Shema*? For if the
truth of monotheism could be learned in a flash, Judaism
would be open to the objection that it is trivial. After one or
two elementary lessons, its teachings would be exhausted.

By arguing that the Torah is an educational vehicle,
Maimonides is arguing that the proper understanding of
monotheism is a life-long process. To learn and fully appreciate the meaning of the *Shema* may require considerable
mental exertion. Yet surely this exertion is an obligation
which every Jew must seek to fulfill. If people died for the
principle expressed by these words, those who have the
opportunity to think ought to devote themselves to uncover-
ing it. If they do, one thing will become clear: The battle
against idolatry continues to be fought. In the ancient world,
the temptation was to worship pieces of clay, wood, and
stone. Today this temptation no longer exists. Not even the
most wayward Jew is inclined to Baal worship. Should we
therefore conclude that idolatry is no longer a possibility?
According to Maimonides, the lessons of monotheism are not

limited to the ancient world; they are eternal truths, and idolatry an eternal temptation. Worshipping pieces of clay represents one form of idolatry, but hardly the only one. So modern Jews cannot congratulate themselves because there are no idols in their houses and think themselves free from any taint of idolatry. Maimonides thinks that Judaism involves more than a body of ritual; the ritual has a purpose, to bring us to an understanding of God and His unity.

In every age Judaism requires exertion. It sets itself in opposition to ignorance and intellectual complacency. On these matters, *idolatry* is just another name for *ignorance*, from which it follows that ignorance is intolerable. Someone who cannot distinguish Judaism from single-deity paganism, or who has not made the effort, has accepted the Torah merely as a set of arbitrary injunctions, not as an educational vehicle.

2. Why Does the Bible Depict God in Anthropomorphic Terms?

In the early part of the twentieth century, another Jewish philosopher, Hermann Cohen, suggested that the essential feature of monotheism is not that there is only one God but that the one God is unique. By *unique* he means that God is unlike and therefore not comparable to anything else in the universe; in short, God is and will always remain in a category by Himself. As Isaiah says 40:25: "To whom then will you liken Me, that I should be equal?" If we suppose that Athena is the only god, she is not unique in this sense of the term because she can easily be compared to a human being. She has a body and wears clothes like a human being, has human emotions and human fears. In fact, she is nothing but a human being glorified. According to Cohen, the distinguishing feature of monotheism is not an arithmetic point (one as opposed to 12) but a qualitative point (incomparable as opposed to comparable). To the degree that single-deity paganism conceives of god as a glorified human being, it remains pagan. The intellectual revolution that is Judaism consists in the realization that God bears no resemblance to a human being, an animal, a natural object, or a natural force, which is why it is forbidden to depict God in any of these forms. God is separate from, superior to, and utterly unlike anything in His creation. To be sure, there is only one thing that is separate in this way: God. He is in the most literal sense of the term *kadosh*. In Maimonides, we find variations on the same theme.

According to Maimonides, to say that God is one is to say that He is a perfect unity, that He does not admit any form of plurality. This means that He does not have parts: a front and a back, a body and a soul, a beginning and an end, a formal or a material component. The God of Judaism admits of no duality whatever. At *Guide* 1.51, Maimonides writes:

> ... there is no oneness at all except in believing that there is one simple essence in which there is no complexity or multiplicity of notions, but one notion only; so that from whatever angle you regard it and from whatever point of view you consider it, you will find that it is one, not divided in any way and by any cause into two notions ...

If God does not admit complexity or multiplicity, He cannot resemble a corporeal object. Anything corporeal can be divided into parts: left and right, front and back, beginning and end. So any attempt to think of God in corporeal terms is bound to fail. He has no height, breadth, or weight; He does not occupy space and experiences neither generation nor corruption. Like Cohen, Maimonides insists that God is in a category by Himself, a category which cannot be depicted in graven images.

It is sometimes objected that Maimonides' conception of God makes Him too distant from human beings, too abstract. According to this objection, people find it difficult to believe in something incorporeal. They need a material image of God on which to focus. As one person put it: "You cannot pray to nothing at all." What is needed, so the objection runs, is some way to bring God down into the world, to bridge the gulf that separates God from His creation. There is a respect in which Maimonides would be sympathetic to this criticism. There is a powerful tendency to think that only things we can see and touch are real. How can we deny the existence of something right in front of us? It is precisely this tendency that gives idolatry its eternal appeal. Idolatry provides concrete images of the divine, tangible subjects to pray to. The pagan gods were thought to eat with mortals, cohabit with mortals, and direct the flow of mortal events. Some of the mystery religions of ancient Greece believed that the deity was devoured by his worshippers and entered their bodies in a literal way. Thus, the worshipper is led to believe that the deity is really there, really affecting his or her life.

A lesser thinker than Maimonides might have argued that while other peoples require a material image to believe in, Jews do not. It is important to recognize, however, that this is not Maimonides' position. Jews are as prone to materialism as anyone else. Hence the repeated instances in the Bible in which Jews, having been warned of the folly of idolatrous worship, continue to pursue it anyway. Powerful as this tendency is, Maimonides is certain it must be overcome. The significance of the Torah is that it provides the intellectual wherewithal with which to overcome it. At *Guide* 3.29, Maimonides credits Abraham with the discovery that God is neither a body nor a force residing in a body, that God is always at a distance from material things. Here *distant* is another name for *unique*, itself a synonym for *incomparable*. To insist on the incomparability of God, then, is to reject the pagan worldview. The rigor of Maimonides' position on the uniqueness of God bespeaks his utter revulsion with paganism. Throughout *The Guide*, he rejects attempts to bring God down into the world by identifying a feature He has in common with it. A common feature or bond other than the ability to reason is, according to Maimonides, a conceptual impossibility. At *Guide* 1.52, he claims there is neither a relation nor a correlation between God and the world He has fashioned, the difference between God and His creation being not one of degree but of kind.

If this is so, the respect in which monotheism differs from single deity paganism has been solved. But this solution underscores the difficulty of another—how God is depicted in the sacred writings of Judaism—for these writings undoubtedly portray God in anthropomorphic terms. Some people think that in order to be committed Jews, we must believe that everything the Torah says is literally true. Recall that for Maimonides, it *is* true. The question is: Is it true in a literal sense? Does one affirm Judaism or, ironically, reject it when one insists that God *literally* walked with Noah, spoke to Moses, or descended on Mt. Sinai? The crux of Maimonides' argument is that literal interpretation of such passages does not indicate authentic Judaism but its opposite. If every word of the Torah is literally true, God might as well be living on Mt. Olympus.

Why, then, does the Torah contain such language? Why should a sacred work not strive for literal truth? The short answer to these questions is that the transition from paganism to monotheism is among the most abrupt one can make. If the transition were simply an arithmetic one, moving from multiple-deity paganism to single-, there would be no problem. Because the real transition (to move from a god who is comparable to things in the world to a God who is not) is more difficult, it cannot be performed in a day. It requires nothing less than an intellectual metamorphosis. Mindful of these considerations, Maimonides argues at *Guide* 3.32 that it would have been impossible for the ancient Jews to have been given a body of law that moves from paganism to monotheism all at once: "For a sudden transition from one opposite to another is impossible. And therefore man, according to his nature, is not capable of abandoning suddenly all to which he was accustomed." The people would not have been ready for monotheism and might well have rejected it. As he points out again and again, the Torah speaks the language of ordinary men and women. But ordinary men and women cannot think in the abstract terms suitable to a philosophic treatise. It is not surprising, therefore, that the Torah often makes God a character in a narrative and speaks of Him in corporeal terms. Nor is it surprising that the prophets use parables or similes to make clear their meanings. If they had spoken in a technical vocabulary, few would have understood them.

Consider a related case. A beginning physics student is learning about electricity. We could present the student with a set of equations, but if we did, we would probably generate more confusion than understanding. So we start with a simile. To understand electricity, think of water flowing through a tube. We can ask about how much water is flowing or how much pressure the water exerts against the side of the tube. The pressure corresponds to volts, the amount of water flowing to watts. The comparison is imperfect, but it is enough for the beginning student to get started. In Maimonides' view, the narratives and parables in which God is depicted in anthropomorphic terms serve a similar function. They are part of an educational process whose purpose is not to deceive the audience but to facilitate the transition from paganism to monotheism.

Much more needs to be said. In particular, we need to know how the passages mentioned above are to be interpreted and what the details of a monotheistic conception of God are. Can a monotheistic God create a world, or is the world, like God, eternal? Are we to believe biblical accounts of miracles or prophecy? How can He issue commandments? Are there reasons for what God commands? Perplexities remain, but intellectual perplexity is not necessarily a bad thing. In some instances, it leads to confusion; in others, it provides the motivation that is needed for the soul to discard old beliefs and look at the world in a whole new way. The purpose of *The Guide* is to resolve as many of these perplexities as possible. We are now in a better position to see what these perplexities are and why they are important.

3. *How to Study the Guide*

This book is not intended to be the last word on Maimonides' philosophy. It is an introduction, a way of starting to think about the issues he discusses. It should be understood that the interpretation of great philosophers is always controversial. If great philosophers bid us think about the world in a new way, they have to devise their own manner of speaking and pursue previously untraveled avenues of thought, and therefore sometimes they stammer. Sometimes they hesitate to take paths they themselves have opened up. Even the tidiest of thinkers sometimes leave loose ends. Scholars can spend a lifetime trying to clear up those issues. One should not get the impression that Maimonides' thought is so simple or obviously true as to be beyond question. Still, the study of Maimonides, or any great philosopher, must begin somewhere. There is no point in focusing on the anomalies and loose ends first.

There is a further reason why the interpretation of Maimonides is difficult. Consider two ways in which accumulation of knowledge can proceed. The first takes as its model the science of geometry. Axioms and postulates are introduced which remain unchanged for the life of the inquiry. In this way, the axioms and postulates serve as a kind of logical foundation. It is from this foundation that we deduce the body of theorems which make up the subject matter of the science. The goal of the inquiry is to see what the axioms and postulates imply.

There is, however, a different way to proceed. Suppose we begin with basic premises but, unlike the deductive model, allow for the possibility that these premises may have to be changed. It is like a ship that has to be repaired at sea. The crew begins the journey with a certain set of expectations. Some of these expectations prove to be wrong. When the crew realizes a mistake has been made, it takes material from one part of the ship and uses it to fix another. The result is that the ship which reaches the final destination is not altogether the same as the one which set out. Anyone who has ever tried to teach a class to beginning students knows how apt this analogy is. The class starts with beliefs it regards as true, but sooner or later, the beliefs accepted at the outset turn out to be false or misleading. The class must then revise its understanding of the premises it is using. Over the course of its investigation, the class may have to make revisions three or four times. This does not mean that the premises the teacher put forward at the beginning were wrong or that the teacher was being less than honest in suggesting them. They were appropriate given the level of knowledge the students had at the time. The fact that the students came to revise or discard them shows that maturing students may outgrow their original beliefs. This model of accumulating knowledge is often called dialectical.

In the history of philosophy, practitioners have used both deductive and dialectical approaches. Maimonides tells us, in the introduction to *The Guide*, that he is going to proceed in a dialectical fashion. He supposes that his imme-

diate audience is a young disciple who has studied the Torah
and scientific literature but is now in a state of perplexity
because he cannot reconcile them. Maimonides then points
out that in dealing with obscure subjects like God, creation,
or providence, a teacher may have to begin the inquiry with
relaxed standards of rigor. At times, the teacher may have to
appeal to the student's imagination, just as the physics
teacher did by comparing electricity to water. Eventually, the
standards will become more exacting, so that what was said
at the beginning may be modified at a later stage. In the
Introduction, Maimonides writes:

> For there may be a certain obscure matter that is difficult to
> conceive. One has to mention it or to take it as a premise in
> explaining something that is easy to conceive and that by
> rights ought to be taught before the former, since one al-
> ways has to begin with what is easier. The teacher, accord-
> ingly, will have to be lax and, using any means that occur to
> him or gross speculation, will try to make the first matter
> somehow understood. He will not undertake to state the
> matter as it truly is in exact terms, but rather will leave it so
> in accord with the listener's imagination that the latter will
> understand only what he now wants him to understand.
> Afterwards, in the appropriate place, that obscure matter is
> stated in exact terms and explained as it truly is.

There is nothing dishonest about this procedure, but it does
challenge the interpreter to decide when the author is being
lax and when rigorous.

Maimonides can also be difficult to interpret because he
does not believe in spoon-feeding his audience. He tells us
he will *not* say everything that can be said on the subject of
monotheism with absolute clarity. Again, from the introduction to *The Guide*: "A sensible man thus should not demand
of me or hope that when we mention a subject, we shall make
a complete exposition of it, or that when we engage in the
explanation of the parables, we shall set forth exhaustively
all that is expressed in the parable." There are several reasons
for this. In the first place, it is doubtful whether any human
will ever know "everything that can be said on the subject."
Only God can be presumed to know this much. Conse-

quently, throughout *The Guide*, Maimonides emphasizes the fallibility of human knowledge and the humility with which we readers must approach his investigation. In the second place, Maimonides believes, with Plato, that an important part of the learning process involves the student's coming to understand things for him or herself; in short, learning involves discovery. If the teacher dots all the i's and crosses all the t's, the student never has the opportunity to feel that the knowledge gained is his or her very own. So a teacher who uses the dialectical model points the student in a particular direction but does not lead the student every step of the way. From time to time, such a teacher may present the student with puzzles, speak in an elliptical fashion, or leave only a trail of hints and clues. Such a pedagogical model presents special challenges for the interpreter because it raises the possibility that behind Maimonides' stated position is a secret or esoteric doctrine that few people can comprehend.

Finally, Maimonides is aware of the Talmudic dictum (Hagigah 11b) that esoteric matters should not be discussed in public. While *The Guide* is very much part of the public domain, it does not leave one with the impression that such questions can be resolved quickly. On any reasonable interpretation, then, *The Guide* is an inducement to further reflection.

In dealing with a thinker like Maimonides, interpretation can never be mechanical. One cannot simply paraphrase the text; one has to think the problems through oneself and hope that one has continued in the direction to which Maimonides pointed. It might be said, therefore, that the interpreter always includes a bit of him or herself in the interpretation. The interpretation is really a *theory* of what Maimonides meant and how we should respond to it. There are, of course, good theories and bad; but in the last analysis, there is no substitute for reading the text of *The Guide* oneself.

With these considerations in mind, we embark on the path which Maimonides has set for us. We will find that some of his worldview is no longer accessible to us, e.g., his astronomy or various aspects of his medical theory, but we will also find that his understanding of God and Judaism lays claim to eternal validity. To the degree that Maimonides has uncovered eternal truths, *The Guide* will seem like a compelling book even though more than eight centuries separate its author from his present audience.

CHAPTER TWO

DESCRIBING GOD

Now therefore, I pray Thee, if I have found grace in Thy sight, show me now Thy ways, that I may know Thee . . . And the Lord said unto Moses: "I will do this thing also that thou hast spoken, for thou hast found grace in My sight . . ." And He said: "I will make all My goodness pass before thee . . ." And He said: "Thou canst not see My face, for man shall not see Me and live."

Exodus 33:13-20

DESCRIBING
GOD

1. Must the Torah Be
Interpreted Literally?

We have seen that the sacred literature of Judaism often describes God in physical terms, and that such descriptions cannot be taken in a literal way. Unless we succumb to the most egregious form of anthropomorphism, we must admit that Noah could not walk with God as he walked with his sons, Moses could not speak to God as he did to Aaron, and God could not sit on a throne as King Solomon did. Accordingly, the first portion of *The Guide* is a catalogue of terms in the Bible which seem to imply that God has human characteristics. In each case, Maimonides argues that while these terms appear to commit the Bible to an anthropomorphic conception of God, in reality they do not. To bolster this argument, he has to engage in a fair amount of textual exegesis. Here are a few examples of what his exegesis is like.

1. IMAGE (*tzelem*). *Genesis* (1:26) does say that man was made in the image of God. If taken literally, this passage would mean that God has two arms, two legs, a face, and hair. But if God looks like a human being, why does Judaism go to such lengths to forbid us from drawing or sculpting Him? To avoid an anthropomorphic conclusion, Maimonides points out that *image* is an ambiguous term (*Guide* 1.1) which sometimes denotes a resemblance in figure or shape. In English, we might say "He is the image of his father," meaning that two people look alike. But sometimes the degree of resem-

blance is much looser. If we say, "He was the very image of valor," no one would argue that valor has arms and legs. According to Maimonides, it is this second use of *image* which is the best approximation of the Biblical claim that man was made in God's image. What the text means is that, unlike anything else on earth, God made us in His image by endowing us with rational faculties. Interpreted this way, Genesis 1:26 is both true and important yet does not imply that there is a physical resemblance between human beings and their Creator.

2. SEE, APPEAR, or LOOK (*raah, hibbit, chazah*). Sometimes, a prophet will say that he saw God in a vision. Earlier we referred to Isaiah's vision at 6:1. Other times, a prophet will say that God appeared to him, as in Genesis 18:1: "And the Lord appeared to Abraham by the terebinths of Mamre." In still other cases, the Bible claims that God Himself saw something. If God has no shape, no one can see Him in the way they see corporeal things; by the same token, if God has no body, *He* does not "see" by virtue of sense organs. Maimonides shows that *see* and related terms are also ambiguous (*Guide* 1.4). In English, we speak of seeing with our mind's eye as a way of meaning we understand something; thus: "After much discussion, I finally see your point." In many languages, *see* and its equivalents can be used in a figurative or abstract way. At Ecclesiastes 1:16, the author claims: "Yea, my heart hath seen much of wisdom and knowledge." Maimonides argues that whenever God "sees" or "is seen" in the Bible, the seeing involved is of this type. The prophet who "sees" God is really thinking about Him, and God's "seeing" is His contemplation of the world. In neither case does the Bible mean that God has a body with sense organs.

3. THRONE (*kisse*). The Bible contains many references to the throne of God. According to Maimonides, this "throne" is a literary device used to convey God's exalted dignity or moral position (*Guide* 1.9). The Bible is simply telling us that God is the supreme authority in the universe. It is not saying that He actually sits in a chair. When the Bible says that God is sitting (e.g., Psalms 123:1), it means that God is permanent and unchanging. The same thing is meant when it describes God as *dwelling* somewhere.

4. TO GO UP (*alah*), TO GO DOWN (*yarad*). Here, too, the words in question are ambiguous both in Hebrew and in other languages (*Guide* 1.10). Sometimes *up* and *down* refer to spatial location, but other times they refer to rank or position, as in, "He ascended to the Presidency." In other contexts, such terms refer to intellectual accomplishments, as in, "She is ready to move on to higher mathematics," or "This material is so elementary, it is surely beneath her." In the Bible, God is said to *descend* when He is ready to reveal something to a prophet, as in Exodus 19:20: "And the Lord came down upon Mt. Sinai." God is said to *ascend* when the revelation is completed, as in Genesis 17:22: "And God went up from Abraham." This is a way of explaining that God has come to the prophet in a vision and that such a vision is of finite duration. We should not try to picture God moving from heaven to earth and back as an elevator moves from one floor to another.

5. TO COME NEAR (*karav*). To say that God is near to those who call upon Him (Psalm 145:18) is to speak about intellectual comprehension, not physical location (*Guide* 1.18). The same applies to words which suggest that people can touch or approach God. They *approach* God in the way one approaches the understanding of a principle or idea. Thus, a person might say, "Scientists are getting closer and closer to a cure for this disease." What is meant is that their ideas are becoming clearer and their theories more comprehensive.

6. TO SPEAK (*amar*). God does not have a mouth or utter sounds. A person who attempted to record God's communication with Abraham or Moses would hear nothing. The hundreds of passages which say "and God spoke" are using figurative language to mean "and God willed" (*Guide* 1.65). By virtue of superior understanding of God, the prophet is able to understand what God wants us to do, which is to say, what God commands. These commandments need not be transmitted by sound waves in the air. Similarly, God's hearing is another word for His comprehending it (*Guide* 1.45).

2. But We Want
the Real Torah Back

From these examples it is clear that the drift of Maimonides' exegesis is to make the relationship between God and His prophets an intellectual one. Maimonides is one in a long line of Jewish commentators who have proposed rationalistic interpretations of Scripture. Thus, words denoting place, sight, hearing, or position are interpreted as mental properties or dispositions. In our own vocabulary, it could be said that Maimonides has attempted to demythologize biblical narrative. Instead of a God who dwells in heaven, sits on a throne, visits earth, and utters sounds, we are given a God who is a perfect intelligence. Instead of prophets who are visited by God in a literal way, we are given prophets who understand what God wants for the world.

A common objection to Maimonides is that "demythologized" Torah is unsatisfying. According to these people, Torah is the literal word of God; therefore it should be taken to mean exactly what it says. By interpreting everything in terms of mental properties or dispositions, Maimonides is replacing the "real" Torah with a human version. To the people who voice this objection, biblical narrative loses its hold on us if it is nothing but a collection of literary devices whose purpose is to underscore philosophic truths. They want God to be a direct participant in the story, much as Athena is a direct participant in the *Iliad* and the *Odyssey*. In short, they want God physically to enter the tent of meeting, utter audible sounds, and show His face.

To such people Maimonides would point out that there is always a feeling of loss when we begin to look at things in a critical way. A child who looks in awe at a rainbow will find out that it is only a phenomenon caused by the refraction of light. American schoolchildren are first told that the Civil War was fought over a moral issue — slavery — but if they pursue their education, they will subsequently learn that economic issues like tariffs played important roles as well. So the Bible is not the only subject in which more learning produces a sense of disquiet. Maimonides would insist, nonetheless, that the desire to make God a direct participant in the story, to conceive of His role in the Bible as we conceive of Athena's in the *Iliad*, is part of the lure of idolatry. At *Guide* 1.36, he goes so far as to say that belief in the corporeality of God is worse than idolatry, as the latter term is normally understood.

His hope is that eventually the need to hold on to a naïve view of God will subside as more questions are raised about His unity. If the naïve view of Torah seems more satisfying at first, this impression is likely to be short-lived. Its appeal is to the imagination, not the intellect. The problem is that naïve interpretations will not carry us very far. We could not do modern physics if we continued to think of electricity as water flowing through a tube, or higher mathematics if we continued to think of numbers as little sticks to be moved from one pile to the next. If we were to use appeal to the imagination as the sole criterion, we would prevent ourselves from making intellectual progress. The last resort of those who want God to be a direct participant in the story is to insist in a dogmatic way that the Torah depicts Him that way. The reply is, again, that the Torah depicts Him that way only if interpreted in a literal fashion. Maimonides' point is that such literal interpretation flies in the face of our ability to make sense of monotheism and the meaning of the *Shema*.

3. What Is a Monotheistic Understanding of God?

Having rejected a naïve understanding of God, we must ask what a sophisticated one is like. In view of Maimonides' shift from the physical to the intellectual, we might expect that God is a necessary being with infinite knowledge and power. This expectation is borne out in the early part of Book Two, when Maimonides tries to prove that God exists. Historically, proofs of the existence of God have not played as important a role in Jewish philosophy as they have in Christian. From a Jewish perspective, it is as if a person who requires a proof to believe in God has missed the point of the religion. Still, there is no question that Judaism is committed to God's existence, and Maimonides offers a number of arguments to

show why this belief is compelling. The simplest of his arguments goes as follows.

The universe is not empty; we can at least be sure that
the things we perceive with our senses exist. We can explain
the existence of these things in one of three ways: (1) All
things are eternal and exist necessarily, (2) Nothing is eternal
and exists necessarily, (3) Some things are eternal and exist
necessarily, some things not. According to Maimonides, the
first explanation is obviously wrong: we see things come into
existence at one moment, perish at another. The second case
is also wrong. If nothing were permanent, it is conceivable
that everything might perish and nothing take its place.
Maimonides objects that the idea of an empty universe is
absurd. So a necessary Being is needed to insure that the
universe does not become depleted. This Being cannot derive
its existence from an external source, because if it did, its
existence would no longer be necessary; it would owe its
existence to something else. Therefore the necessary Being
must be independent of everything else. Maimonides thinks
it is impossible for two things each to exist independently,
because they would have to share a common nature or
essence: independent existence. To the degree they shared
it, they would be part of a larger whole and no longer independent. Maimonides therefore concludes that only one
Being derives its existence from itself, and this Being is God.

Since God is self-caused, everything that derives its existence from an external source must ultimately derive its
existence from God. We may think of this in the following
way. Suppose one is stopped at a train crossing watching a
long series of boxcars roll by. Each boxcar is pulled along by
the car in front of it. In this situation, it would be reasonable
to conclude that the train cannot consist entirely of boxcars.
Since each boxcar is moved by something else, one car — the
engine — must be able to move itself. Without the engine, the
rest of the train would come to a stop. By the same token, if
every being in the universe derives its existence from an
external source, one Being must be the source of its own
existence. Without such a Being, the universe would contain
nothing.

If God is the source of all existence, then God can know everything in the universe by virtue of knowing Himself. This is not true of finite beings. I am not the cause of the table I see in front of me, which means I have to confront it as an external object. I cannot learn about it by closing my eyes and thinking about myself. I have to open my eyes and perform a careful examination. But since God has created everything in heaven and earth, nothing exists independent of Him. To know something, He has only to ask Himself what He created. Notice that both of these features — God's being self-caused and God's ability to know all things by knowing Himself — are unique to God, so both features serve to emphasize the fact that He is in a category by Himself.

If God is both the cause of Himself and the cause of everything else, He must have an infinite amount of power. And if the Bible's account of Him is accurate, He must use this power for good ends. Let us now list the things people normally believe to be true of God.

God is.
God is one.
God is self-caused.
God is powerful.
God is wise.
God is good.

In looking over this list, one might be tempted to think that we have the makings of a science of God, a monotheistic theology. It would seem that human reason allows us to demonstrate that certain attributes are true of God, other attributes not. The purpose of such a science would be to identify God's attributes and explain what they mean.

Unfortunately, we have reached another case where our first intuition leads to perplexity. We can think of this like climbing a mountain. We exert ourselves in order to reach a plateau. We can rest on the plateau for a while, but eventually we will see that there are higher peaks to climb, so we will have to exert ourselves again. The first level of exertion was needed to give up literal interpretation of the Torah. We saw that attributes like *is wise* or *is self-caused* are better descriptions of God than are attributes denoting physical location. The present challenge is to see that even attributes like *is wise* or *is self-caused* create problems. The main problem created by these attributes is that they introduce plurality. We saw before that in Maimonides' view, God does not admit plurality in any sense. From whatever way one thinks about Him, God is and must always remain one. Now look at our list. We have ascribed six different things to God: existence, unity, self-causation, power, wisdom, and goodness. If all of these attributes are true of God, one might object that God is not one but six. His nature seems to admit of plurality because there are at least six different descriptions under which He falls.

Another way to see this point is to consider the nature of subject/predicate statements. If we say, "John is tall," we are talking about two things: John and tallness. If we apply the same analysis to God, an immediate problem develops. Consider "God is wise." By analogy with John, it seems we are talking about two things: God and wisdom. If God is one thing, and wisdom another, predicating wisdom of God would be introducing plurality where we do not want to find it. According to *Guide* 1.53: "His essence is . . . one and simple, having no notion that is superadded to it in any respect." The problem is that subject/predicate statements always give us two things. In the case of John, this duality is not troublesome. In the case of God, it is. Any statement about God which implies complexity, either material or grammatical, contradicts Maimonides' claim that from whatever angle you view Him, God is radically one.

Here, then, is a case where we must proceed in a dialectical fashion. We considered one of Maimonides' arguments for God's existence. The argument leaves one with the impression that God possesses multiple attributes. Since this impression must be mistaken, we have no choice but to examine the basic premises of our discussion and ask whether revisions are in order. Specifically, we have two questions: (1) How can a number of different attributes be true of God if He is radically one? (2) How can *any* attribute be true of God if subject and predicate are a grammatical complex composed of two things?

Consider the second question first. How can we commit ourselves to divine unity if the subject/predicate structure of our language always introduces complexity? One answer is to insist that subject and predicate be identical. Suppose we were to limit what we say to "God is God." The problem is that a statement like "God is God" is uninformative. No one would claim that monotheism is nothing more than the belief that God is identical with Himself. That is true of everything in the universe. Another answer is not to make God the subject of a statement at all; in other words, to contemplate God in perfect silence. Interestingly enough, there are passages where Maimonides adopts this view. At *Guide* 1:59, he quotes Psalm 65:12: "Silence is praise to Thee." At the end of the chapter, he quotes Ecclesiastes 5:1: "For God is in heaven and thou upon the earth; therefore let thy words be few." But while this answer may be satisfactory for someone who has climbed to the top of the mountain and can contemplate the perfection of God without uttering a word, it is not satisfactory for those of us still struggling to get there. If we are to learn anything about God, we must find a way to talk about Him without introducing plurality.

4. Can We Know What God Is or Only What He Is Not?

Maimonides' suggestion is that despite the apparent similarity between

John is tall

and:

God is wise,

the statements are quite different. Behind this suggestion is Maimonides' recurrent theme that God is unique, and therefore the categories we use to think about Him must also be unique. We cannot assume that the grammatical structures that apply to finite objects like people also apply to God. Different subjects must be talked about in different ways. Correctly understood, a statement like "God is wise" tells us not what God is but what He is not; it says that God does not have any intellectual deficiencies. By the same token, "God is powerful" is a way of saying that God is not weak or ineffective. Hence we turn all positive statements about God into negations. Positive statements introduce complexity. We begin with God and add another idea like wisdom or power. Negations do not have this additive dimension. Instead of attaching another idea to that of God, negations separate the idea of God and therefore preserve its unique identity. We could introduce a thousand different negations about God and still maintain He is radically one. All we would be saying is that there are a thousand different descriptions under which He does *not* fall. And every one of these negations would be a way of saying He is unique to Himself.

A common reply to Maimonides is that the shift from positive to negative form solves nothing. Let us go back to "John is tall." A person might argue that this statement is equivalent to "John is neither short nor of medium height." In other words, the difference between "God is wise" and "God is not intellectually deficient" is merely stylistic. If all Maimonides has done is to replace one with the other, then, the objection goes, he has not really changed anything. The statement "God is not intellectually deficient" merely says that God has a perfect intelligence. So we are right back to subject/predicate propositions. The shift from positive to negative form is like trying to clean a room by sweeping the dirt under the carpet.

One thing to keep in mind when discussing Maimonides, or any other great philosopher, is that if they do make mistakes, the mistakes are not easy to spot. It is very rare that a great philosopher fails to see something that strikes us as obvious. If there were no real difference between a positive statement like "God is wise" and a negative one like "God is not intellectually deficient," then it would be true that Maimonides' solution is no solution at all. But, again, there is more to the matter than what our first impression suggests. For Maimonides, "God is wise" is correctly analyzed as "God is not intellectually deficient *or* wise in a conventional sense of wisdom." He makes this point at *Guide* 1.58. To say that John is not on the short end of the scale is to put him on the tall end. Here, the positive and negative formulations are equivalent. In the case of God, however, we are saying that

He is not on *either* end of the scale—that He is completely off it. It is not that God is more intelligent than we are, but that His intelligence bears no resemblance to ours. So the difference between God's intelligence and ours is not one of degree but of kind. God's intelligence is so unlike ours that it cannot be measured according to the same criteria. Similarly, God is not on the same scale as we are with respect to power, goodness, unity, or existence. In every case, Maimonides argues that God is radically unlike us, which is the crux of what is termed *negative theology*.

It is important to see that negative theology does not mean a negative attitude toward life. We will see in a later chapter that the love of God is still a real possibility. What is more, it is important to remember that God is the only thing we characterize in terms of what it is not. Everything else can be described in the normal subject/predicate way, so we will not be using negative theology when it comes to prophecy, commandments, or the perfection of the human soul. We use it only when we talk about God as He is in Himself.

Thinking about God in a negative way sometimes leads to paradox. If Maimonides is right, it is *not* true that God is more intelligent than we are, or more powerful, or more benevolent. The reason is that to compare two things, we must have a common measure with which to judge them. We may conclude that Sally is more intelligent than Frank because she always receives higher test scores and better grades in school. Negative theology forbids us to think of God in this fashion. There is no intelligence scale on which He can be rated. His intelligence, power, and benevolence bear no relation to ours—*not even a normal relation of superiority*. At *Guide* 1.56, Maimonides considers the suggestion that God's existence is more durable than ours, His life more permanent, His power greater, and His knowledge more perfect. But he concludes: "... the matter is not so in any respect." There is no comparison between Him and us. Thus the words of Isaiah 40:25: "To whom then will you liken Me?"

We are left with the conclusion that statements ascribing being, unity, self-causation, power, wisdom, and goodness to God are not normal attributions, even though they bear a superficial resemblance to the statements we make about people. In effect, the statements we make about God are ways of getting at the same point: His uniqueness. They tell us that whether we are talking about wisdom, power, goodness, or anything else, God is beyond the categories we use to describe things in the physical world. He is not a bigger, stronger, better, or more intelligent person than we are. This much could have been said about Athena. Rather, He is a being of a completely different order. It may be the case that God's negative attributes are nothing but roads that converge on a single destination. Before we go into this question in more detail, we must make sure the plateau we have just reached offers stable footing.

5. Is God a Complete Mystery to Us?

Sometimes the best way to understand a difficult passage is to focus one's attention on what the author is denying. Just as a coach might get ready for an important game by taking a close look at the other team, so a student can understand a philosopher by considering what his or her opposition would say. To appreciate the view of Maimonides' opponents, consider the following situation. A child is struggling to play a simple tune on the piano. An adult walks into the room and asks, "What are you doing?" The child says, "Playing the piano." The adult replies: "You're not playing the piano. Vladimir Horowitz *played* the piano. You're just pounding out notes."

The point of this example is that a term like *playing the piano* is ambiguous. It can apply to everyone from a concert-hall musician to a neighborhood entertainer to a beginning student. In one sense, all play the piano; in another sense, the concert-hall musician has mastered a skill that the others have not. When a term applies to an ascending scale of achievements, philosophers say that it is predicated *by analogy*. The primary meaning of the term is at the top of the scale; the derivative meanings, further down. According to the philosophic tradition that derives from Aristotle, words like *wisdom, power,* and *goodness* are predicated by analogy as well. The primary instance is God. The derivative instances include angels (if there are any), then humans. We could say that a well-known scholar is wise, but if we did, we would mean that the scholar still falls short of the standard of perfect wisdom represented by the divine mind. This tradition reached its fullest expression in the thought of Thomas Aquinas, the leading Christian philosopher of the Middle Ages. The difference between Maimonides and his opponents is that they think God stands at the top of the scale, while he thinks God is entirely off the scale.

Why does Maimonides insist that God is off the scale? The answer has to do with his conviction that the difference between God and us is one not of degree but of kind. God's intelligence is not just a superior version of ours. It is not just that He can solve more difficult problems than we can and do them in a shorter period of time. By the same token, His power cannot be described in foot-pounds or any other mechanical measurement. One way to see how dissimilar God's intelligence and power are from ours is to go back to the question of attribution. As applied to us, *wisdom* and *power* denote two very different things: One has to do with ability to see relations between concepts, the other with ability to move objects through space. There is no reason to suppose that the two are related. A person of superior intellect may be so frail that getting out of bed is burdensome. A person possessed of enormous strength may be a moron. If we added "goodness" to the list, we would get yet another attribute. Goodness may be connected with intelligence and power, but it is all too easy to think of examples where it is not.

Now consider the following three claims:

God is wise.
God is powerful.
God is good.

According to Maimonides, these claims have to mean the same thing. In God, wisdom, power, and goodness have to be identical. If they were not, we would have three different things predicated of God so that, once again, we would be introducing plurality where it cannot exist. In God, and God alone, all predicates are ways of referring to one basic fact. What is that fact? Maimonides thinks it is God's complete transcendence of anything in this world, His being in a category by Himself. To repeat: *wisdom, power,* and *goodness* when applied to us refer to three different things. But when applied to God, they refer to the same unitary nature (*Guide* 1.57). If so, there is really no relation between the meaning of these words when used in a human context and their meaning when used in a divine one. The contexts are so different that the words take on radically different meanings. According to *Guide* 1.56:

> ... the terms "knowledge," "power," "will," and "life," as applied to Him ... and to all those possessing knowledge, power, will, and life, are purely equivocal, so that their meaning when they are predicated of Him is in no way like their meaning in other applications.

We are left with the conclusion that God is wise, powerful, and good, but not in ways that allow us to assert an analogy between His attributes and ours. Terms are predicated analogously when we are talking about things in the same category. The concert-hall musician and the young child may have vastly different skills in playing the piano, but both are human beings with two hands, two eyes, and two ears. In principle, the child could grow up to become a concert pianist, too. By denying any analogy between us and God, Maimonides argues that we cannot use our intelligence, power, or goodness as a basis for understanding His. We cannot begin with a minimal understanding of intelligence and, like a child practicing the piano, pull ourselves up to the point where we can understand what intelligence is in God. God's intelligence remains radically different from ours no matter how much progress we make as measured in human terms.

It is clear what price Maimonides pays for rejecting the doctrine of analogy. If there is no analogy between God's intelligence, power, and goodness and ours, we have no hope of understanding what these attributes are in God. We can say that they all must be identical or else God's unity would be compromised. But when it comes to how God thinks, how He generates power as a result of thinking, and why His power is necessarily benevolent, the only thing we know is that we cannot know. All we can do is confess ignorance. This is another way of saying that the internal nature of God is and will always remain a mystery. According to *Guide* 1.59: "... none but He Himself can apprehend what He is ... " We cannot even grasp it in the partial way that a child grasps what is needed to be a concert pianist.

Some people object to this conclusion. Why study a subject if all you are going to find out is that you cannot know anything? The answer is that confessions of ignorance can take several forms. When a student admits ignorance of how to solve a geometry problem, we know that with more effort, the outlines of the solution might become clear. If Maimonides' confession of ignorance were of this type, we would be justified in objecting to it. In other cases, a confession of ignorance, the recognition that we *cannot* know something, may be a great achievement. For thousands of years, people worked on the following geometry problem. Given a square with a side of unit length, construct a circle equal in area to the square. This problem, squaring the circle, exercised some of the greatest mathematicians who ever lived. Not until the seventeenth century did someone show the construction to be impossible. Here, the recognition that we do not and never will know something represented a great discovery, for it put centuries of speculation to rest. It could be said, therefore, that the "ignorance" involved in squaring the circle is of a different order from that involved in trying to solve a tough but solvable problem. Let us call the former *learned ignorance*, the latter *simple ignorance*. Maimonides tells us at *Guide* 1.59 that when it comes to God as He is in Himself, how He sees the world and sustains it, learned ignorance is all we can hope to acquire. Like the mathematicians who puzzled about squaring the circle, we will come to the realization that all our attempts to understand the internal nature of God will fail. Only God can understand the nature of God. If so, speculation on what intelligence, power, or goodness are in God is useless. It is an attempt to learn what in principle cannot be known.

The only thing we can say about the nature of God is that whichever way we view it, or in whatever way we describe it, it is off the scale of intelligibility. In one way, this admission says more about us than it does about God. It says that when we try to understand God, we come face to face with our own limitations. That is why Maimonides suggests at *Guide* 1.59 that, rather than talk about God, and give the impression that we understand what we are talking about, it might be wiser to contemplate His perfection in silence. In this instance, silence would be the mark of learned ignorance.

6. How Can We Pray to Something We Cannot Understand?

No matter how sharply we distinguish between learned and simple ignorance, Maimonides cannot end his discussion by proclaiming the divine nature a mystery. If nothing positive can be said of God, if silence is the only option, much of what counts as prayer, worship, or study would be pointless. How could we praise God for being just and merciful if divine justice and mercy are beyond our ability to make sense of them? How can we say that Jewish law is divinely revealed? Put otherwise, if the idea of God were completely mysterious, it would lose much of its religious significance. On the other hand, every time we try to say something positive about God, we run into the problem that subject/predicate statements always introduce plurality. Once again, we seem to be in a quandary.

Maimonides' solution is to direct our attention away from God as He is in Himself to the consequences or effects that flow from Him. The crucial point is this: Although the divine nature can never admit plurality, and therefore cannot be the subject of a normal subject/predicate statement, there is no reason why God cannot have a plurality of effects. With respect to God's effects, the problems we have encountered in the previous two sections vanish.

To make this point, Maimonides offers a helpful comparison (*Guide* 1.53). Imagine that various objects were placed near a fire. The fire might produce very different results in each of them: clay would harden, wax would soften, sugar would turn darker, a number of other chemicals turn lighter. It would be foolish to argue that because the fire had these results, it itself must be black and white, or hard and soft. The fire is a single thing, but it is possible for a single thing to have multiple effects. What person has not wondered how the same book can cause one reader to cry, another to laugh? Maimonides claims that when we talk about God's being merciful, gracious, jealous of His unique status—in short, when we talk about His *moral* qualities—we are really talking about His consequences or effects. God is such that He has beneficent effects on the world. Although these effects are many in number, we cannot suppose that God Himself is many. This inference is just as foolish as the one which holds that the fire is both black and white. In both cases, what is true of the effects—that they are many and various—need not be true of the cause. At *Guide* 1.53, Maimonides tells us:

> It accordingly should not be regarded as inadmissible in reference to God . . . that the diverse actions proceed from one simple essence in which no multiplicity is posited and to which no notion is superadded. Every attribute that is found in the books of the deity . . . is therefore an attribute of His action and not an attribute of His essence . . .

Maimonides goes on to insist that there is a scriptural warrant for this view. In the passage quoted at the beginning of the chapter, Moses says to God: "Show me Thy ways, that I may know Thee." A few lines later, God says to Moses: "Thou canst not see My face, for man shall not see Me and live." Instead of showing His face, God proclaims that He will cause His *goodness* to pass before Moses. At *Guide* 1.54, Maimonides interprets the passage to mean that the injunction against seeing God's face shows that no person can understand God as He is in Himself. So Moses, the greatest of the prophets, had to accept the limitations imposed by the human condition: Not even he could know God as He is in Himself. All of this is compatible with saying that God *did* reveal to Moses the moral qualities with which He is traditionally endowed: justice, mercy, faithfulness, jealousy, etc. What Moses was given, therefore, was a knowledge of God's consequences or effects. This knowledge, although one step removed from God, is all that is needed to make sense of religious worship and practice. We can praise God for His mercy, as long as we realize that mercy is not part of the divine nature itself—for the divine nature can have no parts—but something which flows from God and from which we benefit.

At this point, someone might be inclined once more to introduce the doctrine of analogy. The argument might proceed as follows: Merciful actions spring from human agents when they act on certain character traits or dispositions. Therefore, it is reasonable to assume that if merciful actions flow from God, He must have similar traits or dispositions. Maimonides rejects such a move at *Guide* 1.54. True, the actions which flow from God resemble those just or merciful actions performed by humans, but we cannot assume there is any similarity in the agents who perform them. To be more specific, we cannot assume God acts according to the same responses or dispositions in human beings. If God does not admit plurality, He cannot be subject to a range of feelings or shifting emotional states. According to Maimonides, we have no idea how God produces the just or merciful consequences that flow from Him. It is as if God is a black box. We have some acquaintance with the things that come out of the box, but not with the mechanism by which they are generated.

The only exception to this rule is an issue to be discussed in the next chapter, where we will see there are reasons to think the universe is ruled by a free agent rather than a blind force. Yet Maimonides continues to insist we have no ground for ascribing human motives, responses, or dispositions to God. Even on the issue of freedom, he thinks we cannot know anything about God for certain. The best we can manage is a well-founded presumption. All this is a way of saying that to the degree we know anything about God, our knowledge is indirect. He is not the one who *is* just or merciful as much as the one who *generates* just or merciful effects. On the basis of the passage from *Guide* 1.53 (quoted above), these effects are sometimes referred to as *attributes of action*. Instead of *being* merciful or just, God *acts* to make merciful or just effects occur.

Consider yet another comparison. Imagine the charitable organizations in a community are suffering from lack of funds. One day an anonymous donor makes available large sums of money. Suddenly, the hungry are fed, the homeless sheltered, the sick comforted, the abused protected. As long as the donor remains anonymous, we will never know his or her background and motivation. In that regard, the donor will remain a mystery; yet in another regard, the donor will serve as a model for the rest of the community. It makes perfect sense to describe the donor as just or merciful *if* we mean the donor's actions have brought about just or merciful effects. It is along these lines that we are to conceive of God. We may offer praise and thanksgiving in a straightforward way. What we cannot do is pierce the veil of anonymity which surrounds the inherent nature of God.

7. Let's Be Practical

It is time to take stock again. The passages in the Bible which depict God as sitting on a throne or descending on a mountain cannot be true in a literal sense. If we are to understand the truths such passages contain, we must go beyond the anthropomorphic language to the philosophic point they are trying to make. Though the prophets, the greatest of whom was Moses, achieved a superior understanding of God, this understanding does not concern God as He is in Himself but His consequences or effects. In the Middle Ages, philosophers like Maimonides claimed that God's consequences or effects *emanate* from Him. It is as if God were like an eternal and inexhaustible source of light whose energy is so vast that it nourishes and illuminates everything around us. But even the best scientific theories cannot explain how that light is generated. All we know is that the light makes possible everything we see and do. On the other hand, the light is so brilliant that no person can look at it directly.

Having reached these heights, we are now in a position to appreciate Maimonides' contribution to the understanding of God. When most people think about God, they try to imagine what it would be like to have infinite power or infinite knowledge. They picture themselves being able to move mountains or see through walls. Does this sort of conception help us to know God? Maimonides is convinced that it does not, that it is no more than a ticket to incoherence. He proposes that we not try to ask what the world looks like from God's perspective, nor try to ask how knowledge, power, and goodness, which are three distinct things in us, can be identical in God. One can almost hear Maimonides saying: Do not focus your effort and attention on what you cannot comprehend. At *Guide* 1.32, Maimonides recounts the story of the four rabbis who entered paradise. One died, one went mad, one become an apostate, and one emerged unscathed. He interprets the story as meaning that all four rabbis were exposed to difficult and esoteric subjects. What enabled the one rabbi, Akiba, to remain unscathed is that he was able to recognize his limits as a human being and did not try to overreach them.

We can therefore imagine Maimonides continuing his advice. Recognize that God is completely transcendent; no earthly force or entity can be compared to Him. When dealing with God as He is in Himself, all we can do is admit ignorance and contemplate God in awe. On the positive side, we must focus our effort and attention on the qualities which flow from Him. Think about justice, mercy, feeding the poor, healing the sick, observing the Sabbath, following one's obligations to parents, friends, and civil authorities, respecting the dignity of other parts of God's creation, living in knowledge of and harmony with the forces in one's environment. What is God? He is the one who bids us to perfect our souls and insures that such perfection is possible. When we set out to perfect our souls, we bring our purpose in line with His. But perfecting the human soul does not mean making fruitless attempts to know things beyond our grasp. In this respect, Maimonides is practical. Once we get beyond the existence and unity of a transcendent Being, the only positive knowledge we can have of God is to look at His consequences or effects as a goal at which to aim. The Bible (Leviticus 19:2), asks us to become as much as possible like God. Since there is no analogy between our knowledge or power and His, we cannot imitate God's essence or inherent nature. But if Maimonides is right, we can discipline ourselves so that the effects of our actions resemble the effects of His. If God heals, we may heal; if God is gracious, we may be gracious; if God loves the stranger, so may we. Thus *Guide* 1.54: "For the utmost virtue of man is to become like unto Him . . . as far as he is able; which means that we should make our actions like unto His . . ." The advantage of moving from concern with the nature of God to concern with the things which flow from Him is that we replace useless speculation with a program for human behavior.

Consider Moses. According to Maimonides, Moses' understanding of God was greater than that of any human being who ever lived or ever will live. What did this understanding culminate in—a metaphysical treatise? an invitation to think about infinite knowledge or power? No. Moses' understanding culminated in a body of law, a code of conduct, which is to say a series of challenges. The law also helps to instill correct opinions, but these opinions are always within the scope of what we can understand. So if one gets the impression that Maimonides downplays speculation, that he always has his eye on the ethical implications of believing in a transcendent God, the impression is justified. A rabbi and a physician himself, Maimonides was directly involved with efforts to improve the human condition. He was convinced that those efforts are the way to reach an understanding of God—or as much of an understanding as human beings can achieve. One can almost picture him declaring: God is the one whose actions lead to mercy and justice — that is all ye know on earth, and all ye need to know.

CHAPTER THREE

CREATION

In the beginning God created the heaven and the earth. Now the earth was unformed and void, and darkness fell upon the face of the deep; and the spirit of God hovered over the face of the waters. And God said: "Let there be light." And there was light.

Genesis 1:1–3

CREATION

1. What Happened in the Beginning?

The previous chapter dealt with God, what He is, and what we can say about Him. We saw that the primary way we have of describing God is indirect: in terms of His consequences or effects. In moving from God to the rest of the universe, we must now ask: What account of creation is compatible with a God who is known to us as a being from whom beneficent consequences flow? Here, as before, we will soon find that human knowledge is limited. Just as we cannot know God as He is in Himself, we cannot know precisely what took place in the first instant of time. No one can fathom what it is like to bring whole galaxies into existence. The issue is rather: Can we interpret the opening lines of Genesis as an extension of the view we have been developing? Is there any moral significance which attaches to the idea of a creating God?

At *Guide* 2.13, Maimonides describes three positions people take on creation: One originates with Moses, one with Plato, and still another with Aristotle. Let us take them up in order.

Moses. The theory ascribed to Moses and to the Torah holds that at one point, there was nothing in the universe except God. God then brought everything else into existence. This theory is often referred to as creation *ex nihilo* or creation *out of nothing*, because it says that in the beginning, there was God and nothing else. The entire universe was brought into being by an act of divine will: "Let there be . . ." What the theory of creation *ex nihilo* denies is that God created the universe from pre-existing materials. When a sculptor makes a statue, or a builder constructs a house, creative activity requires raw materials — marble or clay in one instance, bricks, wood, and glass in the other. So neither the sculptor nor the builder creates in an absolute sense; instead they cut, shape, or mold what is already there. To create in an absolute sense, they would have to begin with no materials and produce a finished piece of work merely by saying "Let there be . . ." Clearly no finite creator can do this; no human being can make something out of nothing. The only agent who can create in an absolute sense is God. The reason for this is simple. It requires a finite amount of energy to cut, shape, or mold pre-existing things; it requires infinite energy to create from nothing at all. According to the theory of Moses, the creation of the universe is unique. The activities of sculptors and builders involve *change* in the order of existing things. God's activity involves the radical *origin* of existing things. Once again, God is off the scale. He is not merely a sculptor or builder of a grand sort. Unlike their creations, His cannot be duplicated.

Plato. The theory ascribed to Plato holds that God *is* like a sculptor or builder on a grand scale. According to the Platonic view, it is impossible to make something from nothing. God can do anything that is within the realm of rational possibility, but not even He can create without some kind of pre-existing material. Hence, God must have created the universe out of a formless stuff, a primordial matter lacking any definite quality or shape until God gave it one. Creation, then, is the act of giving shape or form to this matter. Before creation, something existed, but in an amorphous or chaotic state. By an act of will, God brought order to the world. It is still true that God must have infinite creative energy, because we are not talking about making a statue but about creating the entire cosmos. What the Platonic theory denies is that God's creative energy is so great that He can dispense with any material component.

Aristotle. The theory Maimonides ascribes to Aristotle holds that while the universe depends on God for its existence, it is eternal and therefore never was created. This theory is the ancient equivalent of what is now called the "steady state" hypothesis. God always was and always will be; consequently God's creative energy always was and will be expended. If so, the universe is as everlasting as God. To the question, "What happened in the beginning?" the Aristotelian answer is: There never was a beginning.

According to Maimonides, the Aristotelian theory is committed to more than just the eternity of the universe. It is committed to a universe that operates according to a fixed and unyielding pattern, a universe without free will. There is some question whether Aristotle really denied free will, but we are here considering not what Aristotle said but what Maimonides ascribed to him. To understand why Maimonides thought Aristotle denied free will, note that as we normally use the term, *free will* presupposes the ability to change one's mind. Suppose there are two ways to reach a destination: a scenic way and a fast way. If I am a free agent, then, having chosen one, I am at liberty to change my mind and choose the other. With respect to God and creation, the ability to change implies that at one moment there is no universe, then God decides to change this situation and bring the universe into being. This change of mind is said to constitute an instance of Divine volition. Maimonides' position is that by denying creation, the Aristotelians also deny that God can do anything different from what He has always done. In short, the Aristotelians maintain that God is invariant and can never initiate new action.

The crux of the Aristotelian argument is that change, and therefore free will, is incompatible with the conception of a perfect being. If something is already in a perfect state, if it is not striving to attain perfection but has already achieved it, change would involve deterioration. If God is perfect, there is no superior condition to which a change could take Him. Thus, the Aristotelians argue that God's activity is constant, and His perfection is completely actualized; He has no decisions to consider, no potential to develop.

Maimonides' account of the Aristotelian argument continues with the idea that God is unchanging. It is from God that the universe derives its existence. What derives its existence from an unchanging source must itself be unchanging. For where would any impetus for change originate? It follows, then, that the laws that govern natural phenomena are fixed and invariant. Individual animals and plants spring from seeds, flourish, and die. But overall the universe remains the same for eternity. The significance of a steady-state universe for religion is that if God and the universe are both unchanging, there is no room for divine intervention. All natural phenomena must follow a necessary course, and God cannot change this course in the least. At *Guide* 2.22, Maimonides maintains that according to the Aristotelians, God cannot intervene in a matter so small as changing the size of a fly's wing. No will, not even the will of God, can alter what has been and must always take place.

Although each of these theories has certain disadvantages, none of them is patently false. Each provides a coherent account of the relation between God and the universe. On the other hand, it is clear that of all the theories, the Aristotelian is the hardest to reconcile with the Bible. The simplest reading of the biblical narrative is that the universe was created, and that having created it, God is free to make changes when it suits Him. The Aristotelian theory denies this possibility. It describes a universe in which divine volition and divine providence are illusory. And by denying free will to God, it undermines the view according to which God is a moral exemplar we must strive to imitate.

With respect to the theories of Moses and Plato, the biblical narrative is ambiguous. In one respect, the Bible appears to confirm the view of Plato. The opening of Genesis says that the earth was in an unformed and chaotic state and also speaks of a pre-existing body of water. God introduces order and makes distinctions. There is no reference to creation out of nothing. At Genesis 2.7, God forms man out of the dust of the ground. In other respects, however, the Genesis appears to confirm the view of Moses. The Hebrew word *bara* (to create) conveys this meaning only with reference to God; when humans create, a different word is used (*yatzar*). One might therefore conclude that divine creation is different in kind from human creation. The text supports this idea by the peculiar way in which it describes God's creative activity. There is no evidence of exertion or duration. God simply says "Let there be . . ." and instantly it is so. No sculptor or builder can work this way. Thus, it is unclear whether the Bible is committed to a theory of creation *ex nihilo* or to some version of Platonism.

Once again we are perplexed and must proceed in a dialectical fashion. Since the text can be read in various ways, we must consider in greater detail the advantages of each. But we must keep in mind Maimonides' insistence that the sacred literature of Judaism is an educational vehicle. Its purpose is to teach us something. As such, it makes a claim to truth. The question is: How do we uncover the truth that the creation story contains?

2. Can the Bible Be Interpreted Scientifically?

We saw in the previous section that the Aristotelian theory has one big drawback: It depicts a universe in which everything happens by necessity. In such a world, God cannot alter the flow of events by working miracles, so one way to argue against it would be to say: (1) The Bible is a true account of what happened in antiquity, (2) The Bible claims that miracles occurred, therefore (3) If the Aristotelian theory denies the possibility of miracles, it must be false. Another way to look at this is to see that if one could show that a miracle has in fact occurred, there might be reason to think that the world is ruled by a God who exercises free choice, for what is a miracle if not an interruption of the natural order — an instance of God exercising free will? It is significant that Maimonides does *not* take this approach. He does not argue that the existence of miracles proves conclusively that the Aristotelian theory is false.

Why not? The most plausible answer is that Maimonides did not believe miracles provide a secure foundation upon which to construct an argument. In some instances, he casts doubt on the Bible's account of miracles, suggesting that what seems like a miracle was really a dream or vision (e.g., *Guide* 2.35 and 2.42). In other instances, he suggests that what appear to be miracles are really part of the natural order and could be accounted for if our knowledge of the natural order were greater (*Guide* 2.29). To take an obvious example, a person living before the twentieth century might have regarded it as miraculous if a hunk of metal were suddenly to vault into the air and fly away. But with greater knowledge at our disposal, we can see this as a perfectly normal phenomenon: the takeoff of an airplane. Maimonides expresses sympathy with the view that all miracles in the Bible might be explained in a similar way. We may conclude, therefore, that Maimonides' rationalism makes him reluctant to stress the miraculous. As a physician of considerable reputation, he had more confidence in those who study the natural order than in those who think they see sudden, inexplicable violations of it.

Another strategy he might have used against the Aristotelian theory is an appeal to religious fundamentalism. Thus: (1) The Bible asserts creation, (2) The Aristotelian theory denies it, (3) Anything that contradicts the Bible is false, therefore (4) The Aristotelian theory is false. But Maimonides is too sophisticated a thinker to believe that the Bible must always be read in a literal fashion. There are numerous passages which imply that God has arms and legs. Rational argument offers convincing reasons why these passages should not be read that way. Consistency demands that we say the same thing about the opening lines of Genesis. A literal interpretation implies that God created the world. At *Guide* 2.25, Maimonides admits that if rational argument shows such a literal interpretation unacceptable, we must look for other ways to make sense of the text. In short, the question of whether the Aristotelian theory is correct cannot be decided on the basis of a simple reading of three verses. Scientific evidence has to be considered and detailed arguments advanced. Maimonides could not have known about the big-bang theory or the steady-state alternative, but the spirit of his thought is very much in the direction of taking scientific results seriously. He would have little sympathy with those who want to ignore scientific conclusions to cling to an uncritical reading of the Bible.

Clearly, Maimonides does not throw the Aristotelian theory out of court. He does his best to state it fairly and rejects simplistic attempts to refute it. He recognizes that the people who believe it are intelligent. In fact, he is so open-minded about it that some scholars think he is actually committed to a version of the Aristotelian position. A more credible reading is that he treats the Aristotelian theory with patience and care. Even though he does not accept it, he thinks something will be gained by asking why other people take it seriously. To demonstrate why the Aristotelian argument falls short, Maimonides must show why it is reasonable to ascribe free will to God. To understand Maimonides' arguments, we will first have to look at the world through the eyes of a medieval astronomer.

3. Do the Heavens Move in Perfect Order?

Medieval astronomers were convinced that the heavenly bodies move in circles. One can form a fairly good idea of this movement by imagining an old-fashioned dance hall in which little points of light are carried around on a rotating sphere above the floor. To the people below, it seems as if one is outside on a starry night watching the passage of celestial bodies. To understand Maimonides' view of the heavens, suppose that the sphere which carries these points of light is an animate being composed of a unique heavenly material. Suppose, too, that there are other spheres that carry the moon, the sun, and the planets. The problem is that it is very difficult to account for the orbits of the planets by circular motion alone. From our standpoint on earth, the planets seem to follow a zig-zag pattern, and sometimes even to double back on themselves. Hence their name *planets*, which in Greek means wanderers. To account for this apparently chaotic motion, some astronomers believed that there was a sphere rotating within a sphere, and in some cases, a sphere within a sphere within a sphere. Aristotle supposed that 55 spheres were needed to account for planetary phenomena visible to the naked eye. Ptolemy supposed that the planets move in a circle around a point which itself moves in a circular orbit outside the earth. Although the number and nature of planetary orbits was disputed, all the accounts of the heavenly bodies were exceedingly cumbersome.

At *Guide* 2.6, Maimonides follows a number of medieval thinkers in claiming that there is an intelligence corresponding to each sphere and that these intelligences are what the Bible refers to as angels. With this picture of the heavens in mind, he makes several arguments on behalf of creation, some positive (creation is the best explanation of the world as we know it), some negative (the arguments against creation are not very good). We will consider one of each type.

The positive argument is that there is too much diversity in the movements of the heavenly bodies to suppose that everything derives from an eternal, unchanging source. If God is perfect and His activity constant, we would expect the heavenly bodies to follow an orderly pattern, everything moving at the same speed and in the same direction. Astronomical observation makes clear that this is not the case: Speed and direction of the spheres vary considerably. Maimonides concludes that the best explanation for this variation is that a God possessing free will created the heavenly bodies in a pattern which suited Him, so that instead of a fixed and necessary order, we have evidence of volition.

Maimonides' argument is not entirely persuasive, a fact he himself recognizes. It assumes that if God were unchanging, we would see nothing but orderly motion in the skies. The obvious response to Maimonides' contention is: If there is no apparent order in the motion of the heavenly bodies, it is because the science of astronomy is still developing. When astronomy becomes more advanced, what looks like diversity to us may later be seen as unified motion. The sphere-withina-sphere idea — an obvious instance of disorder — was, of course, replaced by the Copernican unified elliptical orbit. Though Maimonides has cast doubt on the Aristotelian theory, he has not completely overturned it.

Maimonides' second argument concerns the issue of change in God. It is true, he claims, that change in God would imply lack of perfection if the circumstances of divine action were like the circumstances of human action (*Guide* 2.18). In human beings, the transition from inaction to action is usually brought about by change in environment. A person who is resting becomes thirsty, gets up, and pours a glass of water. A person who is sleeping hears the doorbell ring, awakens, and greets a friend. If we think of change in God as being caused by similar factors, then, from what we can tell, change would imply imperfection. It would give us a picture of a God who has needs, wants, and desires like those of humans. If God is supposed to have infinite creative energy, this picture is impossible.

But, Maimonides insists, instead of thinking of God as *responding* to external conditions, let us think of Him as *instigating* them. Unlike human beings, God does not adapt Himself to changes in the environment. Before creation, there was no environment for Him to adapt to. If God instigates a change, the explanation is not to be found in the universe around Him but in the dictates of His own volition. In other words, the only thing that can bring about a change in God's will is that will itself. If God decided to create the world at a particular time, the decision to act at that moment was always a part of God's providence and is entirely His own doing. If this account is right, it need not follow that God has moved from a perfect to an imperfect state. All we need to say is that God's eternal perfection includes and has always included a time in which He will instigate creative activity.

From Maimonides' standpoint, the Aristotelians have made the same mistake all over again. They have assumed that there is an analogy between God's decisions and ours. If such an analogy were valid, creation would be impossible. Yet, having rejected the doctrine of analogy in his discussion of God's attributes, Maimonides also rejects it here. If God's decisions are *self*-motivated, free will in God need not imply lack of perfection. It is worth mentioning that the opening lines of Genesis do not say that God created the universe in order to realize an external result. All they say is that He created it. If Maimonides is right, nothing prevents us from looking upon creation as an exercise of divine will.

Like the first objection to the Aristotelian theory, this one is not entirely persuasive. Maimonides does not actually prove that God has free will; all he shows is that nothing prevents us from thinking so. Maimonides has demonstrated that the Aristotelian arguments *against* creation are not decisive. A God who can initiate action from which beneficent consequences flow is a reasonable possibility, but Maimonides has not shown that such a God is necessary. Because we cannot know God as He is in Himself, there is still room for doubt, there is still a chance that the Aristotelian view is correct. Maimonides does not achieve, nor does he claim to achieve, the certainty of a geometric demonstration. He admits at *Guide* 2.16 that rather than prove creation beyond a shadow of a doubt, he has only tipped the scales in favor of it.

No matter what strategy Maimonides uses, there is a respect in which he is operating at a disadvantage. If we cannot know God as He is in Himself, we cannot know for sure whether He exercises free will and is capable of instigating change. We can know and admire the effects which flow from God, and Maimonides thinks it is reasonable to believe that these effects originate in a will that is in some sense free. He believes this because he wants to preserve the idea that God is a moral exemplar. In keeping with his negative theology, however, he cannot claim absolute certainty for his position. As we have seen, the idea that creation, or the other beneficial consequences which flow from God, derive from a free will can never be more than a well-founded presumption, the best of several competing hypotheses.

Why can one not prove creation for certain? At *Guide* 2.17, Maimonides points out that from knowledge of a thing as it is at present, it is all but impossible to deduce the circumstances of its origin. He asks us to suppose that a man born with normal health is taken away from his mother when a few months old, then raised by his father on an isolated island. Suppose, too, that he never came in contact with a woman. If we told him how reproduction and gestation occur, he might not believe us. He might point out that human beings have to eat, drink, breathe, and eliminate, and might be very skeptical of the claim that a fetus performs these functions inside the mother's womb. Maimonides uses this example to argue that the principles which explain the developed state of an organism are not necessarily the same as those which explain its birth. He concludes: "No inference can be drawn in any respect from the nature of a thing after it has been generated, has attained its final state, and has achieved stability in its most perfect state, to the state of that thing while it moved toward being generated." If this is true of a single creature, how much truer it is about the whole universe. It follows that whenever we talk about the origin of the universe, we leave the realm of certainty to enter that of probability.

4. All This and We Still Are Not Sure?

At this point, it is reasonable for one to feel a certain amount of disappointment. Why bother with all this theorizing if, by Maimonides' own admission, he has done no more than tip the scales in favor of creation? And, if we take seriously the results of the previous chapter, we can *never* do more than this. To know for certain that God created the universe out of free will, we would have to know exactly how God acts. If, as Maimonides insists, we cannot know the details of divine action but only their consequences or effects, we can never be in a position to speak with certainty.

To the average person, such a conclusion is not very appealing. We feel that if we invest the time to learn something, we want to emerge from the inquiry with definite answers. The truth is, however, that Maimonides' conclusion — that we cannot know about creation with certainty — is often regarded as his most significant philosophic achievement, and in some respects, its full significance was not appreciated until the European Enlightenment, a movement which reached its peak 600 years later.

Maimonides' conclusion was so important because it represents a case of extraordinary intellectual courage. Creation is not an isolated issue. It goes hand in hand with miracles, commandments, and the rest of the biblical worldview. Like any Jewish thinker, Maimonides was strongly motivated to try to prove that creation is necessary. Many before him offered such proofs, claiming that the issue was resolved. In a part of *The Guide* we are not discussing, Maimonides examines proofs *for* creation and finds them lacking. He would like to be able to resolve the issue, to say with certainty that God created the universe, but intellectual honesty prevents him from doing so. The philosopher in him keeps saying that arguments on behalf of creation are not strong enough for the issue to be decided beyond a shadow of a doubt. The easy way out would have been for Maimonides to compromise his standards. If you want to prove something, and your arguments are not decisive, then claim more for them than they actually demonstrate. Claim you have resolved the issue even though your conscience says you have not. Whatever else one may think of Maimonides' philosophy, one must admire the objectivity he brought to this question, for he refuses to claim more for his arguments than what the philosopher in him says they demonstrate.

Intellectual honesty raises an important religious question. The most natural reading of the Bible favors creation. Does God expect us to persuade ourselves that creation is necessary when our own reason tells us otherwise? Or does God want us to be as scrupulous in religious matters as we are in others? Maimonides chooses the second alternative. If the Torah is intended to educate us, it demands that we apply the highest standards and greatest rigor in evaluating our theories. In effect, Maimonides has struck a blow against religious dogmatism, for if he is right, the person who recognizes that certainty in these matters is beyond human intellectual capacity is more honest than the person who claims to know for sure (*Guide* 2.16). It is as if Maimonides is telling us that God is averse to fanaticism. He wants us to explore the issues as best we can and be honest about what we have accomplished.

During the European Enlightenment, the limits of human knowledge became one of the most hotly debated issues. What, if anything, can humans prove about God, creation, or the immortality of the soul? Can these things be known with certainty, or must we ultimately accept them on some kind of faith? We should keep in mind that Enlightenment thinkers were looking back at hundreds of years of religious war and intolerance. Thousands of people, many of them Jews, were killed or tortured because they did not assent to theories the authorities claimed were true or insisted upon as dogmas. That is why the Enlightenment thinkers asked: Can *anyone* know these matters for certain? Increasingly, people came to see that the answer is no. The moral implications of this insight are obvious: If you cannot know definitely about God, creation, and the soul, you have no right to make war on or persecute people who disagree with you. Believe what your tradition tells you, but remember that believing is a long way from proving.

Maimonides' view of religious toleration is not as liberal as those of Spinoza, Locke, Kant, or other key thinkers of the Enlightenment. From our perspective, his position on heresy is unduly severe. Still, Maimonides planted the seeds of toleration by arguing that even though he is committed to creation, commitment is not the same as proof. At *Guide* 1.33, he claims: ". . . The intellects of human beings have a limit at which they stop." That limit must be taken seriously. We may ask whether the universe is eternal or created, but if we respect these limits, we cannot know either one with certainty. This does not mean that Maimonides has made a *leap of faith* as that phrase is normally understood. There are good arguments in favor of creation, but they fall short of scientific demonstration. To Maimonides' credit, although 800 years have passed since publication of *The Guide*, we still do not know for certain whether the world was created or always existed in a steady state. What Maimonides showed is that even without certain knowledge, it is reasonable to believe in creation. On the basis of such rational belief his interpretation of Judaism stands.

5. *What Difference Does Creation Make?*

We have again reached a place where it is helpful to take stock. Maimonides believes he has defended creation as well as it can be defended. Creation is taken to mean that God has free will. If God has free will and is responsible for the universe, He can endow humans with free will, too. It is but a short step from this conclusion to the notion of a God who issues commandments. Commandments generally take the form "Thou shalt . . ." or "Thou shalt not . . ." and would be pointless unless the recipient were free to accept them or reject them. One does not give commandments to inanimate objects, plants, or lowly forms of animal life. But neither would it make sense to proclaim commandments in a universe ruled by cosmic determinism. Why tell human beings it is right to do this and wrong to do that if they do not have the ability to redirect the course of their actions? In rejecting the determinism of medieval Aristotelianism, Maimonides does more than support a particular view of God. He has opened the door to free will *in the universe*; in particular, he has laid a foundation for ideas like commandment, sin, and redemption, ideas without which Judaism would be unintelligible. When Maimonides says that the Aristotelian theory destroys the foundation of the law (*Guide* 2.25), what he means is that determinism destroys the basis on which one being (God) can reasonably exhort another being (humans) to make the world a better place.

Recall that Maimonides listed three positions people take on creation: one associated with Moses, one with Plato, and one with Aristotle. We have discussed the Aristotelian theory at length. What about the other two? Each of the other two accepts the idea of a creating God. Where they disagree is on what creation is like. The theory ascribed to Moses claims that God created the universe out of nothing, initiating His creative activity in a context of total emptiness. The theory attributed to Plato claims God's actions wrought changes in a pre-existing material. Maimonides is not completely clear on which theory he prefers. Most of his intellectual fire is directed against the Aristotelian theory, but the perceptive reader will notice that his arguments work as well for creation out of nothing as for creation out of a pre-existing material. What is more, Maimonides' description of the pre-existing material is so vague that it is difficult to know just what he has in mind. Toward the end of his discussion of creation (*Guide* 2.25), he admits that *either* the Mosaic theory or the Platonic one would preserve the foundation of Jewish law. If so, the choice between them is not nearly so important as the choice between determinism and free will.

There is, however, one consideration which suggests that Maimonides is committed to the Platonic theory. Both the Aristotelian theory and its Mosaic counterpart represent extremes: one denies creation; the other posits creation out of radical nothingness. The Platonic theory is something of a compromise. There *is* creation, but *not* out of nothing. At another place in *The Guide* (2.32), Maimonides claims that people's views of prophecy are similar to those they take on creation. After all, prophecy, insofar as it concerns itself with human behavior, must also concern itself with freedom. Not surprisingly, he then proceeds to discuss three theories of prophecy and to opt for the middle or compromise view. The fact that he does so raises a number of questions. Do his real sympathies also belong with the compromise view on creation, namely Plato's? Is it possible that Maimonides would favor a theory other than the one he attributes to Moses? Or, since both preserve free will and both are plausible interpretations of the opening lines of Genesis, does he leave it to the reader to decide which is right? Scholars are not sure Maimonides' thought contains a loose end here, and the conclusion we are left with is that *some* form of creation is needed to uphold the law, but which one is not clear.

Loose ends leave one unsettled and make it hard to arrive at an overall evaluation of a philosopher's work. One of Maimonides' immediate successors, Gersonides, opted for the Platonic alternative. On the other hand, most religious thinkers since the Middle Ages have chosen some version of creation out of nothing, because they point out that if there were pre-existing material out of which God made the universe, this material would not owe its existence to God. It might owe its shape or form to God, but not the mere fact that it is. They then argue that a monotheistic conception of God requires us to say that everything in the universe owes its existence to God. God is crea*tor*, everything else is crea*ted*; therefore, there can be no material that exists alongside God at the moment He begins to create. There are passages where Maimonides seems to take this position. At *Guide* 2.29, for example, he says: "...that which exists has had a beginning, and at first nothing at all existed except God." But scholars are still unsure whether *nothing* means radical nothingness or nothing definite, nothing fully formed. The former interpretation supports the Mosaic theory, the latter the Platonic.

In evaluating Maimonides' contribution, it would be best to focus on the issue of free will, for in his opinion free will preserves the foundation of the law. Throughout *The Guide*, Maimonides has his eye on Jewish law and the behavior it enjoins. In the previous chapter, we saw that our central way of conceiving of God is as a moral agent. He is the One who bids us feed the poor, heal the sick, observe the Sabbath, honor father and mother, perfect our intellectual capacities. In philosophic terms, this means that existence is not ultimate. Behind the birth, maturation, and death of individual organisms, the change of seasons, the motions of the heavenly bodies, is the God who wills all of it to be. Behind existence and superior to existence is freedom. This, in a nutshell, is Maimonides' view of creation. Freedom expresses itself in the form of commandments which call on us to improve the world we inhabit, to assist God in the act of creation. Since Maimonides focuses on the law, we cannot evaluate his discussion of creation without asking what his understanding of the law is. Everything in *The Guide* hinges on his ability to show that the law makes sense.

6. If God Created the Universe, Why Does the Universe Contain Evil?

A frequent objection to theistic accounts of creation is that the universe contains too much evil to have been created by an all-knowing, all-powerful, and benevolent God. If the universe represents the best work of which God is capable, why are there earthquakes, floods, crop failures, and wars? Why do good people suffer awful diseases or misfortunes? Although Maimonides does not take up these questions until Book Three of *The Guide*, for our purposes it is better to consider them now.

Maimonides' treatment of evil (*Guide* 3.8–13) is influenced by a long tradition of neo-Platonic philosophers according to whom evil is a lack or privation. An agent creates only when he or she produces something positive. Consider an example. If a person takes a lump of clay and shapes a statue, then something positive—a new work of art—has been produced. But if someone else smashes the statue into a thousand pieces, nothing has been created. We might say that the second person "created" a mess on the floor, but this obscures the real point: Creation is a constructive, not a destructive, process. By the same token, it would be misleading to say that someone created darkness by blowing out a candle or created death by committing a murder. Disorder, darkness, and death are not positive qualities but the *absence* of them. The neo-Platonic position says that evil should be understood in the same way: as the absence of something positive. In this respect, evil does not exist in its own right and requires no act of creation. According to Genesis 1:31, "God saw everything that He had made, and, behold, it was very good."

Why, then, does evil occur? According to Maimonides (*Guide* 3.10), the answer has to do with the fact that the universe God created has a material component. Only one thing in the universe can be unqualifiedly perfect : God. If there is going to be a universe at all, it will have to admit of certain imperfections. If, as modern astronomy tells us, the earth revolves on its axis, only half of it can receive sunlight at any given time; the other half must experience darkness. If mountains are washed by rain, the rocks that compose them will be eaten away. If plants and animals are to make room for new offspring, they must grow old and die. So it is true that the universe contains a certain amount of darkness, disorder, and death. Maimonides would point out that these consequences are the price we pay for having a universe at all. Is God responsible for darkness, disorder, and death? Maimonides' reply is: yes, but not *directly* responsible. God's intention was to create an orderly and bountiful material universe. Since it is impossible to have such a universe without the imperfections inherent in material things, it may be said that He created those imperfections in an accidental or indirect way. Thus, the words of *Guide* 3.10:

> . . . it may in no way be said of God . . . that He produces evil in an essential act; I mean that He . . . has a primary intention to produce evil. This cannot be correct. Rather all His acts . . . are an absolute good; for He only produces being, and all being is a good. On the other hand, all evils are privations with which an act is only connected in the way we have explained: namely, through the fact that God has brought matter into existence provided with the nature it has . . .

In this respect, God "creates" evil only in the way that a doctor who performs surgery on a sick patient "creates" pain. The doctor does not operate in order to produce pain. Rather, the pain of surgery is a necessary consequence of what the doctor does try to produce: health.

Maimonides distinguishes three sorts of evil which afflict human beings (*Guide* 3.12). The first is caused by the fact that we have material bodies which are subject to generation and destruction, so that no human being can completely avoid pain, sickness and eventual death. We may prolong life and, according to Jewish law, are obliged to do so, but decay and destruction are inevitable consequences of being born. The second sort are those evils people inflict on other people: murder, robbery, cruelty, injustice. Maimonides believes that all these result from a single privation which we have in our power to correct: ignorance (*Guide* 3.11). The third sort of evil is what we inflict on ourselves by laziness, greed, or self-deception. These arise from ignorance and are also in our power to correct.

As a final point, Maimonides insists that the universe does not exist for *our* sake (*Guide* 3.13–14), but is a vast place created by God in which human beings occupy only a small niche. According to modern science, that place is much larger than anyone in the twelfth century imagined and is ruled by scientific laws describing forces far beyond human control. Maimonides argues that God contemplates the universe from the standpoint of eternal laws, and to think He is directly responsible for events like rainstorms, traffic mishaps, or crop failures is sheer folly. Such occurrences result from natural forces which apply to all of created existence. We may try to lessen the impact of those forces, or heal those who have been smitten by them, but we ought not imagine that God, like some cosmic stage director, is "behind" every misfortune. Maimonides is saying that we must get over the habit of thinking that everything in the universe revolves around us. We must try to look at the universe from a perspective according to which the pains and sorrows we feel do not negate the splendor of whole galaxies, or the magnificence of creation.

Is his theory adequate? In one respect, no. However glorious the galaxies may be, pain and sorrow come to specific people, and the universe as a whole seems irrelevant to a person who has just lost a loved one. To the question "Why must this happen to *me*?" Maimonides has no ready-made answer, but neither does anyone else. No one has a satisfactory explanation of all human tragedies. To put the blame on God is to succumb to ignorance. If an innocent person is stricken with a lethal illness, God is not trying to punish the victim or the mourners. We must seek the explanation of the tragedy in the material conditions which brought it about. Beyond that, we must be honest with ourselves: We do not know why any person in the prime of life has to die or what purpose this death serves. In another respect, Maimonides may have understood something very important about human psychology. The Jewish prayer for the dead, the *Kaddish*, never explicitly mentions death. Instead of allowing the mourner to wallow in sorrow or protest that a loved one has been taken away, the *Kaddish* is an ode to the eternal glory of God: "Magnified and sanctified be Thy great name . . ." Instead of anger, the prayer expresses a continuity with past and future generations, a feeling that though fleeting, our moments on earth are meaningful.

A person unfamiliar with the Jewish ritual of mourning might conclude that the prayer is an evasion, but centuries of experience prove the opposite. The prayer has offered consolation to millions of people from both secular and religious backgrounds. The fact that it has done so is evidence that Maimonides' view of human suffering is not to be taken lightly. There is real psychological value in asking people to look beyond their sorrow and offer praise to God. Nothing can take away the loss we feel when a loved one meets with death. Yet the perspective Maimonides urges on us does have this virtue: It enables us to bear that loss and still retain a measure of dignity.

7. If the Universe Was Created, Could It Be Destroyed?

One more point needs to be clarified. Some thinkers argue that the universe is like a child. Having once been created, it pursues a life of its own, a life independent of God. Maimonides takes issue with this view on the grounds that if God has the power to create the universe, He also has the power to destroy it (*Guide* 2.19 and 2.29). If the universe depends on God's will to come into existence, it depends on His will to *remain* in existence. To be sure, Maimonides thinks God will sustain the universe forever. To understand this point is to see that creation alone is not enough. If the universe is to exist through time, God must both create and sustain it. In later ages, God's decision to sustain the universe was interpreted as a decision to create it anew; in other words, God must constantly *re*create the universe to keep it from perishing. Jewish tradition also maintains that God renews the work of creation. Thus, the words of the morning service: "In Thy goodness Thou renew the work of creation day by day forever." According to the view we are now considering, God renews the work of creation instant after instant; in short, He never stops. So creation is not a one-time-only event. God is as active now as He was in the beginning of time.

Contrary to what some of Maimonides' predecessors seemed to think, continuous creation does not imply that it is a waste of time to look for causal regularities between one moment and the next. Maimonides never doubts that the material world follows a pattern which science can comprehend. What the theory of continuous creation asserts is that this pattern is a consequence of the eternal will of God. The natural order goes on because God continues to sustain it.

The view of continuous creation worked out by later thinkers is a bit more explicit than the one Maimonides adopts in *The Guide,* but it represents a direction in which he clearly wanted to move. It maintains that the universe is radically dependent on God, that the universe cannot sustain itself for a second without the effects of God's activity. There is no question that Maimonides thought of God as an infinite source of creative energy. He would add that while we cannot speak with certainty, we should not think of God as *only* a source of creative energy. God is not forced or constrained to create, nor does He create according to principles imposed on Him by external factors. He creates because He wills to do so. This is the philosophic principle to which Maimonides thinks Judaism is committed.

CHAPTER FOUR

PROPHECY

> *If there arise in the midst of thee a prophet, or a dreamer of dreams — and he give thee a sign or a wonder, and the sign or the wonder come to pass, whereof he spoke unto thee — saying: "Let us go after other gods, which thou hast not known, and let us serve them;" thou shalt not hearken unto the words of that prophet, or unto that dreamer of dreams . . .*

Deuteronomy 13:2–6

PROPHECY

1. Who Is Fit to Be a Prophet?

Having argued that the sacred literature of Judaism is an educational vehicle, Maimonides must say something about the people whose writings and sayings compose the great bulk of it: the prophets. In rough terms, a prophet is anyone addressed by God. In Jewish tradition, there have been both male and female prophets. In either case, we could say that prophecy is the counterpart of revelation. But to say this is to raise a fundamental question: Who are the prophets, and why has God chosen them? Do they have qualifications normal people lack? Can anyone become a prophet? Does God raise up prophets, or do people achieve this state on their own?

We saw that Maimonides thinks people's views on prophecy mirror their views on creation. Not surprisingly, he discusses three positions at *Guide* 2.32: two that represent extremes, one that represents a compromise. The extreme positions correspond to a natural and a supernatural account of prophetic illumination. The compromise position is, in effect, a modified version of naturalism. Since supernaturalism is the easiest to understand, we will take it up first.

According to the supernaturalist, prophecy is a miracle. As a free agent, God can confer the status of prophet on anyone He pleases. It makes no difference whether this individual is ignorant or intelligent, old or young, rich or poor. There is, then, no way to predict who will become a prophet, no way to prepare for the role. The identity of those destined to become prophets is known only to God. In one instance, the prophet may be a prince, in another a priest, in still another a shepherd. All we can say is that God chooses certain individuals to act as messengers to tell the rest of the world what He wants.

The naturalist says the opposite. Prophecy has to do solely with the acquisition of knowledge. It is to be understood along the lines of excellence in physics, mathematics, or other secular subjects. It requires a keen intellect and the personal habits or mental discipline needed to develop that intellect to its fullest. To be sure, it is not easy to become a prophet, but the naturalist insists there is no mystery involved. What prevents most of us from becoming prophets is not that God has decided to raise up someone else but that we lack the necessary qualifications. We cannot become prophets for the same reason we cannot do nuclear physics or higher mathematics: The subject is difficult, and mastery of it too demanding. The naturalist adds, however, that *in principle* there is nothing that stands in the way of mastering any subject we wish.

The third position, modified naturalism, is identical with the previous one except that God cannot turn an ignorant person into a prophet. He can, however, withhold prophecy from someone who, on intellectual grounds alone, may be suited for it. It is clear why the third position is a compromise. The supernaturalist claims that the only thing needed to become a prophet is the will of God; the naturalist claims it is a keen intellect; the modified naturalist claims it is both. For the modified naturalist, a person who wishes to become a prophet must develop his or her intellectual capacities to the fullest *and* hope that God does not step in to prevent the illumination that would otherwise occur.

These issues are important because one's opinion of prophecy is bound to affect one's opinion of the commandments. The laws were given by the greatest prophet of all — Moses — and interpreted by the likes of Samuel, David, Amos, Jeremiah, and Ezekiel. If one takes a supernaturalist position, one is likely to interpret prophecy along the lines of ecstasy or poetic inspiration. Poetic inspiration may seize a person at odd times and in odd ways. The poet may or may not understand the words that come forth. Notice, for example, that poets often speak of being visited by a muse or being a medium for something beyond themselves. It is also well known that poets are not always the best expositors of their own works.

If prophecy is a miracle, and if the prophet need not be a person of superior intellect, there is no reason to expect the sayings of the prophets to form a systematic body of knowledge. Rather than look to physics or mathematics as our model, we would do better to look to creativity in the arts. If so, we are likely to come away with the impression that not all the commandments have a philosophic justification. Few people expect an artist to have a reason for everything, every line, color, note, or word in the composition. The religious equivalent of this position is the view that some commandments must be obeyed merely because God wills them. How do we know God wills them? The prophet, God's official messenger, tells us so. Can the prophet provide a justification? In this view, maybe not. The prophet simply delivers God's message; the prophet may not have the intellectual wherewithal to explain it.

If, however, one defines prophecy in terms of intellectual excellence, the opposite will be true. The commandments will seem like a systematic body of law aiming at the perfection of the human soul. According to the naturalist, no part of the prophet's message can be arbitrary. At no point will the prophet ask us to accept anything whose only justification is "God wills it." Every positive commandment must lead us to some good, every negative one prevent some evil.

It is clear from even the most superficial reading of the Bible that there are passages which lend support to either interpretation. In brief, we have the stories and parables of Genesis, the social and legal codes of Exodus, Leviticus, and Numbers, the beginnings of commentary in Deuteronomy, the histories of Joshua, Judges, and Kings, the poetry of David and the other psalmists, the social criticism of Amos, Isaiah, and Jeremiah, the mystical vision of Ezekiel, and the attempts at philosophic argument in the Book of Job. Since these writings run the gamut from poetry to philosophy, some sort of compromise is needed. Having diminished the importance of miracles in his discussion of creation, Maimonides remains skeptical of miracles here. As is evident from the Deutero- nomy passage quoted at the beginning of this chapter, his skepticism has deep roots in Jewish tradition. Signs and portents, *even ones that come true*, are not sufficient criteria for deciding who is a prophet. Instead, Maimonides identifies prophecy with the highest level of human intellectual achievement. In our terms, prophecy is the crowning glory of a lifetime of scholarship.

In view of the great diversity manifest in the prophetic writings, Maimonides must put forward a broad conception of what intellectual achievement is. He cannot accept either the artistic or the scientific model exclusively. If he did, it would be easy to find passages that refute him.

2. *What Constitutes Intellectual Excellence?*

Let us imagine two different people. The first is an expert in the behavioral sciences. She has studied anthropology, eco- nomics, sociology, psychology, and political science. She is an authority on the civil law and the jurisprudential tradition which interprets it. She can present her knowledge in a coherent and precise way. She can support every contention with argument and evidence. In the field of human behavior, she has reached the pinnacle of intellectual excellence, except that all her knowledge is abstract. She can produce good arguments, but she lacks vision. She cannot give a picture of a world people would be willing to work for, even die for. She is a good teacher, but not a born leader of people; to be a leader, she would need a much more vivid imagination.

The second person is the mirror image of the first. He has an active, vivid imagination. His speeches light a fire in people's hearts. In one sense, he is a dreamer, but a dreamer people are willing to follow. The mental pictures he paints are unforgettable, but he cannot back them up with theoret- ical arguments. He cannot define his terms or provide an- swers to people who ask questions. His knowledge is purely intuitive. What he lacks is a critical understanding of what he is saying.

Each of these people represents a kind of intellectual excellence. The problem is that each also represents an intellectual deficiency. If it is unrealistic to ask people to follow a person with nothing but scientific understanding, it is dangerous to have them follow someone whose only claim to legitimacy is a lively imagination. According to Maimonides, prophecy is that rare case in which a person has both qualities (*Guide* 2.37). The prophet can furnish a vision *and* the theoretical foundations to support it. Maimonides sometimes describes prophecy as an intellectual overflow. In the first instance, he means an overflow from God's mind to the mind of the prophet. We would say that the prophet is not only an intelligent person but someone who has reached a level of genius. In the second instance, the overflow is between scientific understanding and the imagination. It is not only that the person is a genius in the theoretical sense but that the excellence of one kind of knowledge has "spilled over" into the other. Such an individual can visualize the things discussed in theory. According to *Guide* 2.36:

> Know that the true reality and quiddity of prophecy consists in its being an overflow overflowing from God . . . toward the rational faculty in the first place and thereafter toward the imaginative faculty. This is the highest degree of man and the ultimate term of perfection that can exist for his species; and this state is the ultimate term of perfection for the imaginative faculty. This is something that cannot by any means exist in every man.

It could be said, therefore, that prophecy is a kind of illumination in which all aspects of human intellectual capacity work together.

The fact that scientific understanding and imagination work together helps Maimonides explain why some prophetic writings are graphic while others are more abstract. The sacred literature of Judaism contains both in order to appeal to our intellect as well as our hopes, dreams, and fears; it both instructs and inspires. Consider the immortal words of Isaiah 2:4:

> And they shall beat their swords into plowshares,
> And their spears into pruning-hooks;

> Nation shall not lift up sword against nation,
> Neither shall they learn war any more.

Universal peace is a moral ideal that can be defended philosophically, but Isaiah has done more than produce a theoretical argument on its behalf. He has helped us to visualize it. Once heard, his words can never be forgotten; they touch us in a way that argument alone never could. It follows that those who are responsible for prophetic literature must be people of manifold talents.

The obvious conclusion is that Maimonides proposes a compromise: Prophecy is an intellectual act involving two faculties, and on the question of whether it is purely natural or purely supernatural, he opts for the middle position containing elements of both. Since prophecy is an intellectual act, it can come only to a person with superior intellectual gifts and the discipline needed to perfect them. No miracle can turn a fool or even a person of average intelligence into a prophet. On the other hand, God can *prevent* a person with superior intellectual gifts from becoming a prophet. Although it is not clear why God would want to prevent a person of superior intelligence from becoming a prophet, Maimonides seems to think it is possible that He might. So prophecy involves *both* genius *and* the concurrence of God. We can think of this along the lines of people being nominated to an honor society. Only individuals with a long list of accomplishments can get in. The director cannot put forward an undeserving candidate. All the director can do is exercise veto power when an otherwise deserving candidate is found to be lacking something. In this way, the director does not give people something they have not achieved on their own; on the other hand, people need the director's blessing to get in.

If this is so, then, for a person who *does* become a prophet, the experience may to be understood along naturalistic lines. Assuming God does not exercise veto power, the prophet's intellectual development is in principle no different from that of a great scholar or thinker. It is the prophet who is responsible for perfecting his or her native intellectual capacities. There are no shortcuts. One cannot do away with books and study. One cannot go to the mountaintop and expect to receive prophetic illumination on demand. One cannot use prayer to make up for undeveloped talents. True, one must be blessed with native talents in the first place, but the development of these talents requires considerable exertion.

What is more, even when prophetic illumination does occur, the prophet does not go to a majestic location and listen to a mellifluous baritone voice speak from the sky. Even though prophecy involves the concurrence of God, it is not a miracle. It is still true that when the Bible says "God spoke," it means "the prophet understood" (*Guide* 1.65). God does not communicate to the prophet via sound waves in the air. One must never forget that prophecy is an act of intellectual apprehension that cannot be picked up by tape recorders or video equipment. In short, Maimonides' warning about literal interpretation of the Bible still stands.

3. *How Do We Know Someone Is a Prophet?*

The general thrust of Maimonides' thinking is to restrict the sphere of people who are or could become prophets. If prophecy were a miracle, if God could offer the gift of prophecy to anyone He pleases, then the number of potential prophets would be unlimited. On Maimonides' account, this group can contain only people of genius, which is why he says in the passage quoted above: "This is something that cannot by any means exist in every man." The usual criticism of Maimonides' theory is that it is "elitist." If Maimonides is right, most of us can surrender any hope of receiving the kind of prophetic illumination he is talking about.

On the other hand, if Maimonides is right, if the number of potential prophets is highly restricted, we have a good way of closing the door on false prophets. The newspapers are full of accounts of people who believe God has spoken to them. More often than not, the "message" received turns out to be ridiculous or self-serving: God asked me to lie to someone; God told me I deserve a higher salary; God told me I was right to lose my temper; God told me to bet on a certain lottery number; God told me that my neighbor deserved to fall down and break a leg. Maimonides does not doubt that such people have heard voices or experienced vivid dreams. Nor does he doubt that these voices and visions appear to come from an external source. What he doubts is that such experiences have anything to do with prophecy. True prophecy is instructive; it teaches us about God and calls us to our highest moral ideals and aspirations. It is founded on a thorough understanding of the universe and human efforts to grasp the principles that underlie it. A person ignorant of those principles, whose only claim on our attention is an intuitive feeling or dreamlike image, cannot speak for God. Allow such people to determine our religious practices or beliefs and we are certain to get chaos.

What may seem like an elitist theory is in reality a view which asks us to be just as critical in religion as we are in other aspects of our life. No prudent person would accept medical or legal advice from a soothsayer. If we demand intellectual rigor in medicine and law, why should we not also demand it in matters pertaining to God? The truth is that not everyone can be a prophet. Of the many who claim to have experienced prophetic illumination, which ones should we believe? It will not do to take this question lightly. There are people who claim that God told them they deserve a higher salary, but there are also people who claim that God told them to leave bombs in crowded places, to torture heretics, or to assassinate political leaders.

Thus the question "Which of the many people who claim to be prophets should we believe?" becomes "How do we prevent true religion from degenerating into fanaticism?" Recall that Maimonides had firsthand experience of religious intolerance. He knew that Jewish people are not immune to ignorance or superstition. His answer is that our prime criterion for deciding who speaks for God is truth (*Guide* 2.40). If we are presented with a body of law which inculcates true beliefs, which encourages intellectual growth and critical reflection, which makes sound recommendations for personal health and social harmony, then, and only then, do we have a basis for believing that the message may be divinely inspired. So the criteria for deciding who is a prophet are just as rigorous—indeed, more so—than those for evaluating expertise in other walks of life. Although he has a great deal of respect for the powers of the imagination, Maimonides rejects imagination as the sole criterion. In the last analysis, only the most extraordinary individuals have the right to claim that they speak for God. And the only way they can earn this right is to provide both a vision and a rational defense of it. In effect, Maimonides has reversed the normal order of things: The more a person asks us to make leaps of faith, the less likely it is that he or she is carrying a divine message. Signs and portents were rejected as early as Deuteronomy.

On the issue of fanaticism, Maimonides points out in a short work entitled "Eight Chapters" that, according to Mosaic law, God does not want and in many instances will not accept extremist behavior. God does not want people to starve themselves, torment themselves, take vows of celibacy, or endure physical deprivation. What He wants are honest dealings with our fellow human beings, moderation of the passions, respect for the poor, the sick, the widow, the orphan, and the stranger, rest on the Sabbath, and in general a life in which we grow to our fullest potential. To be sure, Mosaic law calls for moral and religious discipline, but it never recommends discipline for the sake of discipline. In every case where a ritual is prescribed or a practice abolished, there is a legitimate reason. The purpose of the law is not to promote unquestioning obedience to authority or to push human beings to the limit of their endurance. It is rather to create an environment in which they can perfect their souls and the society in which they live.

As applied to the coming of the messiah, this theory tells us not to expect faith healing, seances, voices from the sky, the dead coming back to life, or other sensational phenomena. In his other writings, primarily in the *Mishneh Torah*, Maimonides emphasizes that during the days of the messiah, the world will follow its normal course. There will still be rich and poor, strong and weak. The lion will not lie down with the lamb in any but the metaphorical sense. Eventually, the messiah will die a natural death. Rather than a person endowed with superhuman powers, the messiah will be a wise ruler who puts an end to oppression. Since we cannot rely on miracles to identify such a person, we have no choice but to rely on a critical assessment of the messages we receive. Here, too, there are no shortcuts. Rather than look for marvels and miracles, we have to think about the issues and try to become as learned as possible.

4. Will There Ever Be a Prophet as Great as Moses?

Maimonides' theory of prophecy is part of his overall strategy of demythologizing religion. Insofar as we understand prophecy as an act of apprehension rather than a miracle, we open ourselves up to two objections. No one will argue that genius, either theoretical or intuitive, is the sole province of the Jewish people. If Jews do not have a monopoly on physics, mathematics, or philosophy, why should they have one on matters pertaining to religion? If prophecy involves the understanding of important truths, in principle it should be available to the people of every nation. Why should not the people of other religions also have legitimate claims to prophetic illumination? Alternatively, why should there not arise among the Jews a prophet greater than Moses who replaces vast portions of Mosaic law with something superior? Unless these questions are answered, Maimonides' theory would allow for the possibility that Judaism might one day be superseded by another religion, making Judaism's claim to eternal validity hollow.

With respect to gentile prophets, Maimonides appears to think that if a non-Jew perfected his or her soul to the required degree, prophetic illumination would be possible. As one might expect, he does not have a lot to say about gentile prophets, but the category is one he allows. With respect to the second issue, Maimonides follows Jewish tradition (Deuteronomy 34:10) in arguing that Moses' prophecy is unique (*Guide* 2.34–35). In fact, he maintains that the difference between Moses and the other prophets is not one of degree but of kind. The reasons Maimonides sets forth in a variety of writings are as follows. The other prophets did not confront God as directly as Moses did. Thus Moses is the only prophet who spoke to God "face to face" (Exodus 33:11). This does not mean that Moses sat across the table from God, but that Moses achieved a degree of understanding no other prophet did. Other prophets did not come in contact with God as often as Moses did. Other prophets confronted God in dreams, while Moses confronted Him in broad daylight. Other prophets trembled in front of God, while Moses kept his aplomb. Finally, none of the other prophets ever made the claim Moses did: These are the commandments and prohibitions which God gives you. At *Guide* 2.39, Maimonides concludes that the uniqueness of Mosaic prophecy is attested to by the Bible itself.

As it stands, this argument is not altogether convincing. In the first place, it begs the question. Granted that, according to the Bible, Moses is the greatest prophet, is there a philosophic reason to rule out the possibility that at some future date a greater prophet might arise? In the second place, Maimonides is putting forward a view of history few modern thinkers would be willing to accept. For most modern thinkers, human knowledge is cumulative, advancing from one age to the next. We obviously know more about physics, astronomy, medicine, and mathematics than our ancestors did. If prophecy is an act of intellectual comprehension, why should we not know more about religion? And, if we do know more about religion, why should there not arise a prophet whose understanding of God is greater than that of Moses? As Maimonides would have it, human knowledge may make progress, but it will never reach the level attained by a single prophet 1,200 years before the Common Era. To many readers, it seems that, having demythologized the concept of prophecy, Maimonides has now given back some of the ground he previously won. Is his view of Mosaic prophecy not something of a myth itself?

If Maimonides did nothing more to establish the uniqueness of Mosaic prophecy than quote the Bible, the answer would be yes. The truth is, however, that in Book Three of *The Guide*, he reviews every aspect of Mosaic law to demonstrate that it is not just *a* contribution to our understanding of human perfection, but the very foundation of that understanding. Here, it is worth noting that Mosaic law represented a radical departure from other religious codes in the ancient Near East. It rejected ritual murder and ritual magic. It went to great lengths to distinguish murder from accidental homicide and to prohibit the murder of slaves. Sabbath rest, itself a novelty in much of the world, was extended to include not only Jews but strangers living in Israel, slaves, even animals. The Israelite is warned in the strongest terms not to take advantage of the stranger even if the stranger is not a Jew. Consideration for the poor, the sick, and the handicapped is also commanded, but unlike other legal codes which contain such provisions, Moses' puts heavy emphasis on mercy and forgiveness. At Exodus 34:6–7, God describes Himself as merciful, gracious, slow to anger, and forgiving. One would look in vain through the works of Aristotle for similar sentiments. Leviticus 19:18 and 19:34 contain the first known formulations of the Golden Rule: One must love one's neighbor as oneself. In the eighteenth century, Kant maintained that this principle is the basis of all morality, that every moral judgment must be compatible with it and obeyed *because* it is compatible with it. Finally, Mosaic law proscribed the worship of material objects, natural forces, or human beings.

What all this goes to show is that Moses does occupy a unique place in Western moral tradition. Others may have attained a more rigorous or more comprehensive understanding of morality than he did, but it is still possible to assign Moses his preeminence on the ground that he set our moral tradition in motion. Even today, many people, Jewish and gentile alike, would be skeptical of a moral theory which departed radically from the principles Moses first brought to light. They would point out that truth-telling, respect for the dignity of all human life, concern for the less fortunate members of society, and ability to show mercy are basic moral obligations. Should anyone arise to tell us that such obligations can be dispensed with or superseded, we would be justified in treating this individual as a false prophet. Moses' prophecy plays so important a role in our conception of what it means to be a decent human being that we cannot turn our backs on it. We can interpret it, amplify it, or build modern theories around it, but it is difficult to see how we could begin to evaluate human behavior without it.

In the previous chapter, we considered a variant on the theory of creation which went beyond Maimonides' own: that creation never stops. We are now considering an account of Mosaic prophecy which falls short of Maimonides' theory. We have given up the claim that no one will ever achieve an understanding of human behavior superior to, or even on a par with, that of Moses. We have accepted a progressive view of the growth of knowledge. Yet we still have reason to single out Moses for special acclaim. It is still valid to say that though some later thinkers may have gone beyond him, they have stood on Moses' shoulders.

5. Why Must Everything Be So Rational?

We must ask again whether demythologized religion is superior to the kind it is supposed to replace. What have we gained by thinking of prophecy along naturalistic lines? A frequent criticism of Maimonides is that his view of religion is too rational. Some people believe human reason is a rival to God, that the only way we can be true to our tradition is to open ourselves up to the mysterious and the miraculous. Maimonides insists that the opposite is true: Instead of seeing reason as alien to God, so that we are forced to choose between piety and rationality, we should look upon reason as "the image" of the divine in us (*Guide* 1.1). This does not mean we can overcome those limits imposed on our reason by the fact that we are human; rather, it means that only by developing our reason to the fullest can we get as close to God as our natures allow. At the end of the *Guide*, Maimonides asserts that our love of God is identical with our knowledge of Him (*Guide* 3.51), so it is impossible to love God if one is mired in ignorance and superstition. Being open to the mysterious and the miraculous is not sufficient.

Such a view is and will always remain controversial. On the other hand, it is often rejected because of a mistaken impression of what is meant by *reason*. Maimonides' opinion would be ridiculous if he equated reason with mathematical computation. He is not claiming one can reach God in the way one reaches the solution of an algebra problem; for him, reason is not simply a matter of following rules, memorizing formulae, or collecting data. When Maimonides talks about reason, he has in mind a faculty capable of surveying all human experience and discerning in it some purpose or rationale. Reason is not just a faculty of cognition but a commitment to a particular kind of life. Reason requires one to be honest with oneself about what one can know. We do not demonstrate our loyalty to God by being uncritical, by claiming more for our arguments than what they actually prove. It may be said, therefore, that reason imposes a kind of discipline. It also may be said that Maimonides accepts Plato's contention that if reason is a force in the world, it is a gentle one. Developed to its fullest, reason is never harsh, never dogmatic; instead it requires one to treat other people's arguments with patience and understanding, something Maimonides tries to do in his treatment of Aristotle. It requires one to accept criticism of one's own arguments with graciousness. When we talk about the life of reason, we are talking about a way of life in which one's desires are moderated, one's treatment of others is respectful, one's treatment of oneself honest, and one's understanding of the world critical.

For Maimonides, intellectual excellence involves an imaginative as well as a theoretical component. So if we think about reason, we should not necessarily think of modern scholars making technical advances in limited fields of inquiry. A better model would be provided by Maimonides himself: a physician who used his knowledge to heal the sick, a rabbi who put forward a comprehensive understanding of Jewish law, a philosopher who sought to demonstate that Jewish law can be defended in a rigorous and intellectually stimulating way. His life and work are both good illustrations of what Maimonides means by the life of reason, why he thinks it does not get in the way of God. Pursued to its ultimate level, reason will not cause us to reject God but to love Him.

Any mention of the ultimate level of reason takes us back to the subject of prophecy. It should be clear that the prophet has not forsaken the love of God for a metaphysical platitude. According to Maimonides, the rational love of God affects every aspect of a person's behavior. Here, it is important to remember that the Jewish conception of God is action-oriented; the point is not to comprehend the internal nature of God but to understand and eventually to imitate the qualities which flow from it. It is hardly surprising, then, that our record of Moses' prophecy, the Torah, is a guide to all aspects of behavior. In Maimonides' opinion, it puts before us the ideal of the life of reason. Not surprisingly, Maimonides claims at *Guide* 2.40 that a prophet whose own behavior is not in keeping with his message, a prophet who does not practice what he or she preaches, is a fraud and should be disregarded.

It follows that a true prophet is not content with theory alone. A true prophet is a theoretician, but one whose aim is to produce a well-ordered society in which oppression is abolished and citizens are instructed about God, the universe, and the capacity of the human mind to know them. In our terms, the prophet is thinker, teacher, and lawgiver. Taken together, these activities define the rational love of God. They are not only tasks the prophet seeks to perform, but tasks which invariably bring the prophet into contact with other people. Because the prophet loves God, the prophet is committed to improving the lives of others in the community. Private contemplation on a hilltop is part of the prophetic mission, but it can never be the whole of it. Below the hilltop is a city where people must be clothed, fed, housed, encouraged to think critically and worship properly. What motivates the prophet is the hope that the same rational love of God which informs the prophet's actions will inform those of everyone else.

Why then must this love be rational? To insure that it is really God whom we love, not some dangerous and possibly demonic substitute. History is full of individuals who, distrusting reason, followed false gods as a result. Unfortunately, the cost of such mistakes is more than an incorrect opinion; all too often, this opinion takes an enormous toll in human life. So, when someone asks, "Why must everything be so rational?" Maimonides' answer is that reason is our main defense against idolatry. Rationality does not exclude love, dedication, and commitment; what it does exclude are love, dedication, and commitment which are, for all intents and purposes, blind.

CHAPTER FIVE

THE COMMANDMENTS

The law of the Lord is perfect,
restoring the soul;
The testimony of the Lord is sure;
making wise the simple.
The precepts of the Lord are right,
rejoicing the heart;
The commandment of the Lord is pure,
enlightening the eyes.
The fear of the Lord is clean,
enduring forever;
The ordinances of the Lord are true,
they are righteous altogether . . .

Psalms 19:8–10

THE
COMMANDMENTS

1. Must God Be Rational?

Having accepted a naturalistic account of prophecy, we must adopt a similar view of the commandments. We can no longer look upon the commandments as the results of dictation in which God speaks in audible tones which the prophet commits to writing. Commandments originate when the prophet apprehends the kinds of actions needed to perfect the human soul. The usual criticism of such an account is that it robs the commandments of their God-given status. What was once seen as a body of law claiming the full sanction of divine authority is now seen as the product of human understanding. Maimonides would insist, however, that this criticism is off the mark.

We have seen that for Maimonides, reason does not stand between us and God. On the contrary, it is a God-given faculty which, if correctly used, is our sole means of access to Him, or better yet, our sole means of access to that aspect of Him we are capable of understanding. At the heart of Maimonides' account of prophecy is a basic assumption: God wills the perfection of the human soul, which is why the consequences or effects of His activity benefit the human species and provide a standard of morality to which people should aspire. Deny this assumption, and you are denying the sentiments of the 19th Psalm. In Maimonides' opinion, you are also denying much more, the philosophic foundation upon which Jewish law rests. Affirm it, and you are affirming that God's will is not arbitrary. God is not like an arbitrary monarch who acts on whim and forces people to obey rulings they have no hope of understanding. Rather, God is like a ruler who always acts with the best interests of the people in mind and tries to educate them to see what these interests are.

To return to a comparison used earlier, God resembles an anonymous donor who brings beneficial consequences to a community without revealing his or her identity. In such a view, the commandments are ways of working in concert with the donor's intention and helping the community to realize its potential to the fullest. That is why it is impossible for a prophet to be ignorant, for unless a prophet understands the nature of human potential, individually and for the community, the prophet can never understand how to fulfill God's purposes in developing them. Maimonides, consequently, does not think that he is robbing the commandments of their God-given status. On the contrary, any distinction between "God-given" and "contributing to human excellence" he would regard as invalid; whatever falls under one description also falls under the other.

In modern terms, we do not have to compromise human dignity to satisfy ourselves that we are doing God's work. One does not have to be a mystic or guru to claim divine sanction. If Maimonides is right, all the commandments have human excellence as their goal (*Guide* 3.27). No commandment mandates a form of behavior which does not do one of the following: (1) instill a correct opinion, (2) contribute to social harmony, (3) provide for physical or mental health. No commandment is purely revelatory in the sense that the only reason to accept it is God's will. The traditional Jewish position is to follow Leviticus 18:3–5 in distinguishing between two kinds of commandments: ordinances (*mishpatim*) and statutes (*chukkim*). *Mishpatim* are commandments which, if God had not given them to us, we would be justified in establishing on our own. Typical examples include the prohibitions against murder, lying, and adultery. By contrast, the *chukkim* are commandments for which no apparent justification is available. A typical example is the prohibition against eating pork.

Why does Jewish law contain commandments whose justification is not apparent? And why should we obey them? Would it not be more prudent to observe the ordinances and forget about the statutes altogether? We can imagine three ways of approaching these questions. The first says that there is no rationale for the statutes and no need for one. All that matters is that God has commanded us to observe them; everything else is beside the point. The second says that while there are reasons for the statutes, owing to human fallibility we will never know what these reasons are. We therefore have no choice but to observe the statutes as an act of faith. The third says that there are reasons for the statutes, and that we must make every effort to learn what the reasons are.

Maimonides opts for the third alternative. The only difference between the ordinances and the statutes is that the reasons for the former are easier for us to find (*Guide* 3.26). It follows that every ceremony or ritual must serve a purpose. This does not mean that we can know everything about every commandment or that we can stipulate reasons dogmatically. Some of the reasons Maimonides offers are less than compelling. But the search for reasons must go forward even if it cannot be completed in our lifetime.

For Maimonides, then, each commandment is to be viewed as a kernel of wisdom, and thus an intellectual challenge. In support of his position he cites Deuteronomy 4:6–8, the passage quoted at the beginning of chapter one. At *Guide* 3.31, he points out that in this context, the Torah claims *both* the ordinances *and* the statutes are part of the body of wisdom which all the peoples of the earth should be able to admire. If there is a commandment for which no reason can be found, how can it be part of this wisdom? And if no reason can be found for a commandment, on what basis will other people admire it? The conclusion of *Guide* 3.31 is emphatic:

> every *commandment* from among these *six hundred and thirteen commandments* exists either with a view to communicating a correct opinion, or to putting an end to an unhealthy opinion, or to communicating a rule of justice, or to warding off an injustice, or to endowing men with a noble moral quality, or to warning them against an evil moral quality.

Again we are at an impasse. Again we must dig more deeply if we are going to find a resolution. Why did Maimonides depart from some versions of the traditional view? Does he not create difficulties for himself by doing so? Was he aware of these difficulties? To answer these questions, we must first look at how Maimonides sharpens the terms of the debate.

2. Are Reasons Dependent on Context?

With his usual respect for honesty, Maimonides admits two qualifications to his claim that for every commandment there must be a reason. In some cases, a reason may exist for a general practice but not for the degree of specificity we find in the Torah (*Guide* 3.26). Maimonides believes, for example, that there were good reasons in antiquity for the practice of animal sacrifice. But he admits it would be fruitless to try to discover why a ram was needed in one circumstance, a lamb in another. To use a modern example, a person might argue that there must be a cutoff date for paying one's federal income tax, yet this need not imply that there must also be a reason why the date is April 15th instead of April 16th. Once the reason for the general practice is understood, the exact date can be any of a number of possibilities.

The second case is more complicated. We have seen that the commandments exist in order to instill correct opinions, promote social harmony, and provide for physical or mental health. According to Maimonides, however, harmony and health are subordinate to correct opinions (*Guide* 3.27), because the most important feature of the commandments is that they provide instruction. The most important instruction they provide is that God, and only God, is a fit subject of worship. In other words, the main purpose of the commandments is to resist and eventually to overcome the lure of idolatry. Unfortunately, the appeal of idolatry is so pervasive that it cannot be broken all of a sudden. Maimonides is practical enough to realize that if the ancient Israelites were to be weaned away from the religious practices of their neighbors, the process had to be gradual.

If it is asked why the Torah has commandments concerning incense, priestly vestments, and other such items connected with the sanctuary, the answer is that, in ancient times, the people needed visual objects to hold their attention. It would have been ineffective for a prophet to address the people with philosophic arguments and hope to persuade them (*Guide* 3.32). Instead, the people were given spectacles that drew their minds away from idolatrous worship and pointed them in the direction of true religion. This instance is important because it shows Maimonides is not averse to taking into consideration the historical context in which the commandments were given.

To these two instances, let us add a third. In many cases, it is impossible to fulfill a commandment by oneself. One cannot honor a father and mother unless one lives in a community with laws governing marriage and divorce. One cannot refrain from stealing unless there are laws defining property. One cannot distinguish murder from accidental homicide unless there are judicial guidelines to follow and courts to interpret them. One cannot act as a moral agent at all unless there are educational institutions to teach one social and familial obligations. What all of this goes to demonstrate is that morality is a cooperative effort. It requires many people and institutions to succeed; so it is hardly surprising that many commandments are intended more for the community than for the individual.

Notice, however, that once one talks about community or cooperative efforts, one's conclusions cannot have the airtight structure of a geometrical demonstration. Human behavior exhibits regularities and permits one to make generalizations, but the investigation of social structures is not like the bisecting of a line segment. On this point, Maimonides is in sympathy with Aristotle: One cannot expect more precision from a subject than it is capable of providing. It would be just as foolish to demand geometrical rigor from a political leader as it would be to allow political arguments to influence geometry. Accordingly, Maimonides distinguishes between truth and falsity, which can be known with certainty, and goodness and evil, which cannot (*Guide* 1.2).

It follows that whether we are talking about civil or religious authority, the law must address itself to regularities in human behavior rather than exceptions. There will always be a few individuals whose actions are so eccentric or extraordinary that the law does not apply to them. Thus, a law requiring one to give ten percent of one's income to charity would not apply to someone who voluntarily gives fifty percent. Still, the fact that there is an exception does not mean that the law is invalid. At *Guide* 3.34, Maimonides points out that, unlike medicine, the law cannot provide a unique prescription for each person; it must deal with the general rather than the specific.

Why is this important? The answer is that if morality requires a social context and the establishment of social institutions, then it also requires statutory rules or procedures. If there are going to be legislative bodies to make laws, there must be rules for how such bodies operate. If there are going to be courts, there must be rules of evidence and decorum. If there are going to be educational institutions, there must be ceremonies and traditions. So a person seeking to justify a commandment or a particular practice cannot always look at that practice in isolation. To some it may seem there is no justification for having members of the United States Congress address their remarks to the chair rather than to each other. The fact is, however, that this practice is part of normal parliamentary procedure and enables Congress to conduct its business in a civilized way. Although it would be possible to imagine parliamentary bodies using different rules, or perhaps no rules at all, we can still understand that the rules in force are obeyed for good reason. That reason may make sense only in the context of a judicial body; in a normal social setting, addressing one's remarks to a third party would be considered rude.

Similar considerations apply to symbols and ceremonies. Sometimes people need visual images like the flag to inspire a sense of justice, or formal ceremonies to remind them of the importance of their office. The flag might be a different color, and the ceremonies follow a different order. We can admit this and still say that the flag and the ceremony serve a legitimate purpose. The only qualification we must add is that they serve a legitimate purpose provided the government under whose auspices they are used is itself legitimate. No justification can be given for honoring the flag of a tyrannical government. With the exception of the first and second commandments (those relating to idolatry), Maimonides' entire discussion of Jewish law presupposes a social and historical setting.

A final point before moving to the commandments themselves. To say that a rational justification can be found for the commandments is not to say that if one rejects the justification, one is free to reject the commandment. Maimonides never doubts that all the commandments are binding. The purpose of looking for justifications is not to let us decide which commandments to obey and which ones not to obey. It is to enable us to understand what we are doing *when* we obey. Put otherwise, Maimonides wants to convince us that Jewish law is not a hodgepodge of meaningless rituals and prohibitions, but a system of law designed to bring out the best in us. It offers us a picture of human life not only as it is, but as it might become. If some have used the search for reasons as a way of liberalizing Jewish law, this was not Maimonides' intention.

3. What If the Context Changes?

Maimonides divides the commandments into fourteen categories, devoting a chapter to each. This section of *The Guide* calls to mind the comprehensive study of Jewish law he undertakes in the *Mishneh Torah*. We have seen that for Maimonides the ultimate sin is idolatry, the ultimate virtue contemplation of God's eternal and transcendent glory. All the other commandments are means to prevent idolatry or encourage contemplation. Maimonides points out, for example, that we cannot achieve intellectual growth in a lawless or oppressive society. Consequently, there must be commandments which restrict antisocial instincts like greed, envy, hatred, lust, or anger; conversely, there must also be commandments which instill trust and cooperation.

Throughout Book Three of *The Guide*, one cannot help but see glimpses of Maimonides the physician. Left to its own devices, human behavior is prone to excess. The law acts as a corrective which calls on people to moderate their passions, desires, and inclinations; in effect, the law is a kind of medicine that restores balance to a troubled soul. Maimonides has little difficulty showing how the holidays, feasts, and fast days promote a spirit of rejoicing and thanksgiving, or, in other circumstances, promote contrition or repentance. In every case, the law promotes the companionship and cohesion without which a society cannot persist. Maimonides believes that all this is needed if we are to have a society in which people can be guided to truth and spiritual illumination. He demonstrates that many prayers, rituals, and symbols are connected with important doctrines. In addition to providing an opportunity to rest, for example, the Sabbath commemorates the act of creation. Sukkot, Pesach, and Shevuot remind us of the story of the Exodus. Prayers, psalms, and hymns evoke moral emotions like mercy or guide the intellect in its search for God. Repentance allows us to deal with the phenomenon of guilt and to reinstate ourselves in the social order when we have disobeyed its rules.

Maimonides also explains that the Torah prohibits cruelty to animals and indiscriminate killing through the dietary laws, but he is less successful in explaining why foods like pork or shrimp are forbidden. For the most part, the arguments he puts forward are hygienic; the Torah prohibits foods which are unclean, are difficult to digest, or thicken the blood (*Guide* 3.48). That these arguments are based on what now are considered unsupportable medical opinions raises an important question: Might Maimonides' search for reasons produce the opposite effect of what he intended and, instead of reconciling people to the law, turn them away from it? By adducing medical and hygienic reasons for the dietary laws, Maimonides runs the risk that, as medical and hygienic knowledge increases, our opinions about what is a healthy diet will change. Foods once thought to cause harm may be shown to be beneficial. If so, a person who reads Maimonides might be inclined to violate the commandment. On the other hand, if one took the more traditional view, arguing that the only "reason" we are to refrain from pork or shellfish is that God wills it, then medical advances would change nothing, improve nothing.

Maimonides seems to have been aware of this problem but insisted that the search for reasons must go forward.

Although one makes it easy on oneself by using God's will as a reason for a commandment, Maimonides regards this strategy as an abdication of intellectual responsibility. To repeat, he is intent on showing that God's will is fully consonant with human excellence and intellectual development. To do this, he must argue that God's will is never arbitrary, and therefore, if God does not want us to eat pork, we are obliged to seek a rationale.

How can there be such a rationale if the hygienic argument has been discredited? There is no reason to believe Maimonides was anything less than sincere when, in Book Three of *The Guide*, he used the hygienic argument, but neither is there any reason to believe he would continue to defend the argument if medical evidence proved it to be groundless. To defend the commandment in the present age, he would have to shift his emphasis from hygienic considerations to symbolic ones. It may have been true in the past that eating pork was hazardous to one's health. Although a modest amount of it is not considered a medical hazard today, pork has become so strong a symbol of assimilation, and the refusal to eat it so clear an affirmation of Jewish identity, that the commandment still serves a rational purpose; that is, it serves a purpose so long as we recognize what the primary goal of Jewish law is and why continued affirmation of Jewish identity is needed: to overcome the lure of idolatry. Since the other commandments are means to the furtherance of this end, should people lose sight of the end, the other commandments might be brought into question. It is not enough to refrain from forbidden foods; the act of refraining has value only as part of a larger educational process.

Refusal to eat pork can be thereby justified not as an isolated act but as a symbolic gesture which acquires significance as part of a larger religious framework. The Jew who violates the commandment is not like someone who ingests dangerous chemicals, but like the member of a parliamentary body who refuses to obey the rules of decorum and insults other members of the assembly. Insults may not endanger people's lives, but there are good grounds for maintaining that they are harmful to the interests of society because they encourage divisiveness and conflict and should therefore be prohibited.

4. Does Love Require a Reason?

An obvious objection to what we have been saying is that the argument obscures the real point. Maimonides has totally misconceived the love of God. It does not take special conviction to obey a commandment for which there is a convincing justification. The prohibition against eating pork is only one example. Suppose Maimonides is right about pork. Suppose, in other words, that the latest medical evidence shows it leads to intolerably high levels of cholesterol. How would one exhibit love of God by refusing to eat it? All one would exhibit is a desire for self-preservation. Similar considerations apply to the prohibitions against murder, lying, and adultery. These are laws we can justify on our own. To be blunt: We do not need God to see that murder is objectionable. God is needed only when we go *beyond* reason, when we are asked to perform or refrain from acts which we would not think of on our own. Only then can we truly claim that our actions are holy.

To continue this objection, consider the following example. Suppose a husband asks a wife to do something clearly in her best interest: take antibiotics to cure a bacterial infection. It is hard to see how complying with this request could be viewed as an act of love. It is only an instance of common sense. Suppose, on the other hand, that he asks her to do something for which there is no justification: to go walking in the rain without a raincoat. The wife says the idea is ridiculous. The husband says he knows it is ridiculous, but he wants her to do it anyway. The wife refuses. The husband says that if she really loved him, his asking her would be enough. According to the objection to Maimonides we are considering, love requires one to be willing to surrender one's own will to that of the other person, to demonstrate that one is willing to follow the other person anywhere. To keep insisting on a rationale only perverts the nature of love. If we really love God, we should be glad when these commandments have no rationale.

To his credit, Maimonides is not blind to this objection. At *Guide* 3.31, he claims there are people who believe the true test of whether a commandment originates with God is precisely if we can find *no* meaning in it. Maimonides responds in the strongest terms:

> There is a group of human beings who consider it a grievous thing that causes should be given for any law; what would please them most is that the intellect would not find a meaning for the commandments and prohibitions. What compels them to feel thus is a sickness that they find in their souls, a sickness to which they are unable to give utterance and of which they cannot furnish a satisfactory account. For they think that if those laws were useful in this existence and had been given to us for this or that reason, it would be as if they derived from the reflection and the understanding of some intelligent being. If, however, there is a thing for which the intellect could not find any meaning at all and that does not lead to something useful, it indubitably derives from God; for the reflection of man would not lead to such a thing. It is as if according to these people of weak intellects, man were more perfect than his Maker; for man speaks and acts in a manner that leads to some intended end, whereas the deity does not act thus, but commands us to do things that are not useful to us and forbids us to do things that are not harmful to us. But He is far exalted above this; the contrary is the case. . . .

Although his rhetoric may be heated, there can be little question that this issue goes to the heart of Maimonides' understanding of Judaism.

The crux of the objection to Maimonides is that holiness requires surrender to an arbitrary will, only by bending our will to useless commandments do we pay homage to God's superiority. Maimonides replies that exactly the opposite is true: The person who eschews reasons for the commandments makes God seem worse, not better, than human beings. Such a person portrays God as a capricious ruler who, instead of trying to educate the people, tries to make them look ridiculous. It is as if God takes pleasure in watching us set aside our intellectual faculties to engage in pointless, even humiliating behavior.

What would it say about God if He did insist on such pointless behavior? Does the Torah not claim that the commandments were given *for our good* (Deuteronomy 6:24) *so that we may live* (Deuteronomy 30:16)? What is at stake between Maimonides and his opponents is the question of what the commandments are intended to do. Maimonides insists on the assumption which has shaped and directed his entire book: The Torah is an educational vehicle, and every commandment is given for the purpose of teaching us something. To be sure, God wants the pupils to obey. But it does no one any good for the teacher to insist on obedience for the sake of obedience. That is another name for abdication of one's intellectual responsibility. The proper way to pay homage to God's superiority is not to set aside one's intellectual faculties, but to recognize that as a perfect being, God must also be a perfect educator.

In considering Maimonides' position, we should keep in mind that the Torah (Leviticus 19:2) asks us to imitate God. If we picture God as a ruler who issues arbitrary commands which He expects to be followed blindly, we will once again run the risk that the religion we practice might degenerate into fanaticism. The point of Leviticus 19:2 is that worship of God is supposed to call forth the best in human behavior and therefore cannot ask us to set intelligence aside, to stop thinking and just obey. It cannot do this and still claim that the object of our worship is a perfect being. To the husband who says to his wife "If you really loved me, you would do this," the proper reply is "If you really loved me, you would not ask something so unreasonable."

5. What Does It Mean to Love God?

The purpose of Maimonides' discussion of the commandments is to persuade us that they do not originate in an alien will, that they are not rules that force uncharacteristic modes of behavior on a gullible audience. If we take the time to understand them, then, Maimonides insists, we will see that the commandments call for natural behavior which requires what our own best judgment tells us is right. The Torah (Deuteronomy 30:14) claims that the word of God is not in heaven or beyond the sea, but in our mouths and written on our hearts. Maimonides is part of a long line of thinkers who take this passage to mean that an intelligent person can look upon the commandments not as a burden, but as a body of wisdom expressing the true needs of his or her soul (*Guide* 2.39).

Perhaps an example might help. The Fifth Amendment to the United States Constitution makes it illegal for the government to force anyone to testify against him or herself. The amendment was written over 200 years ago by individuals who are long since dead. We might look on this law as the will of strange people who set up a penal system and saw to it that it was enforced. But a study of the history of criminal justice systems would reveal that people have been burned, starved, mutilated, and threatened in order to elicit confessions. In many instances, the torture used to get people to confess to crimes was far more objectionable than the crime being investigated. Anyone who studied this history might easily reach two conclusions: (1) Testimony elicited under torture cannot be reliable, and (2) Quite apart from reliability, on moral grounds alone, torture has no place in a civilized society. To someone who reached these conclusions, the Fifth Amendment is not an arbitrary law handed down by people who lived 200 years ago, but a law we ourselves would institute if we were writing a constitution, a law which, despite its historical origin, expresses our own deepest convictions about how life ought to be lived. In biblical terms, one might say it is a law that is written on our hearts.

Maimonides wants us to think about the commandments as laws we ourselves deeply want. He recognizes that at first a person may not feel this way. To a child just beginning to learn Jewish law, the commandments may seem like a set of needless restrictions, yet a child's immediate intuitions do not reflect the deepest longings of the human soul. Contrary to what popular culture would have us believe, it may require effort, study, and patience to determine what the writing on our heart actually says. Maimonides' position is that if we make this effort, if we knew what the perfection of the human soul consisted of, we would see no real conflict between God's will and our own. We would obey the commandments freely, knowingly, and with conviction. Far from surrendering anything, we would be acting in full possession of our best faculties. We would accept the true opinions inculcated by the Torah, not on faith, but after a long and careful examination of the issues. Then and only then could we say that we really love God. To talk this way is to talk about an ideal of human behavior that few of us realize, because the rational appropriation of the commandments involves nothing less than a complete transformation of the soul, a subject to which we now turn.

CHAPTER SIX

JUDAISM AND THE TRANSFORMATION OF THE HUMAN SOUL

Cast away from you all your transgressions, wherein ye have transgressed; and make you a new heart and a new spirit . . .

Ezekiel 18:31

For my mouth shall utter truth,
And wickedness is an abomination to my lips.
All the words of my mouth are in righteousness,
There is nothing perverse or crooked in them.
They are all plain to him that understandeth,
And right to them that find knowledge.
Receive my instruction, and not silver,
And knowledge rather than choice gold.
For wisdom is better than rubies,
And all things desirable are not to be compared unto her.

Proverbs 8:7–11

JUDAISM AND THE TRANSFORMATION OF THE HUMAN SOUL

1. Whose Religion Is This?

From everything we have seen so far, one thing is clear. The person who begins to read Maimonides, or to think about the implications of his thought, must get over an initial stumbling block. Maimonides' reinterpretation of biblical narrative is so extreme, his reluctance to accept anthropomorphic descriptions of God so unyielding, that, in all likelihood, he is not describing Judaism as practiced by most of its adherents. Many people probably do think of God as a king sitting on a throne, of prophecy as a miracle, and of commandments as ways of submitting to a strange and alien will. If the criterion for evaluating Maimonides' philosophy is sociological—Is this what the majority of Jews actually believe?—our judgment must be negative. But Maimonides is holding up an ideal; his description of Judaism stands to ordinary attitudes as the ideal of a perfect democracy stands to the give-and-take of officials at city hall.

A historian looking at the demographics of a community, or the development of new institutions in it, would want to know what the majority of people think at any given time, but we must be careful not to let sociological considerations steal the show. The Bible records that the history of the Jewish people contains many instances of revolt, frustration, disobedience, and hypocrisy. No sooner were the Israelites freed from bondage than they grew tired of life in the desert and wanted to return to the fleshpots of Egypt. Several

Israelites attempted to revolt against Moses' authority. The episode of the golden calf is one of scores in which the lure of idolatry proved too strong to overcome. The people often insisted on worshipping a god whose image they could see. Immoral practices associated with Canaanite religion found their way into Jewish homes. Political intrigue and assassination plagued the ancient kings. The northern and southern kingdoms plotted against one another. In each of them, religious practices were cheapened and made superficial as people brought elaborate sacrifices to God in the hope that they could go on cheating and oppressing the poor.

It may seem astonishing that all these things happened during eras in which the Jewish people *also* produced the founder of the Western moral tradition and a succession of prophets whose sayings still inspire faith, hope, and courage. The reason is that Moses and the other prophets refused to be content with prevailing attitudes. They saw in Judaism the possibility of changing those attitudes and elevating the Jewish people to a level of spirituality few could imagine. At a time when oppression and inequality threatened the social order, Amos looked forward to an age when righteousness would swell like a mighty stream; at a time when war was imminent, Isaiah foresaw an age of universal peace; amid widespread idolatry, Jeremiah spoke of a new covenant between God and Israel. Yet the Bible tells us that Amos was ordered to leave town, Isaiah's advice was often ignored, and Jeremiah was sent to prison.

Maimonides does not claim to be a prophet, but one will miss the essence of his philosophy unless one understands that, like the prophets, he does not feel bound to accept prevailing attitudes about Jewish thought and practice. He insists on a Judaism which meets the highest standards of intellectual rigor, even if such a version of Judaism should sound strange to the average Jew. In this respect, *The Guide* is *not* intended to be a popular work. It is practical in the sense that Maimonides is concerned with questions of conduct, but it is not practical in the sense that he felt bound to accept circumstances as they are. Some of the rabbis who first read *The Guide* were so outraged they tried to have the book banned. Although not all of Maimonides' opponents resorted to such extreme measures, it is fair to say that *The Guide* ignited a controversy which is still with us: Why do we need philosophic refinements of traditional Judaism?

The answer is that Maimonides believes that philosophy does much more than merely provide technical refinements of traditional religion. Recall that the love of God does not find expression in blind faith or fanaticism. Maimonides claims that the love of God is one with the knowledge of God. If the love of God is to mean anything at all, we must have some idea of what or whom we are loving. If that love is directed to a man sitting on a throne, or the image of one, or a monarch who issues arbitrary commands and cares nothing about the education of his subjects, then, in Maimonides' judgment, it is not God whom we love but some kind of ghastly substitute. If Maimonides is right, love is not a feeling which varies with changes in mood; rather it is an aspiration which brings with it a set of moral and intellectual obligations. That is why, in Judaism, love of God is expressed in the form of a commandment (Deuteronomy 6:5: "Thou shalt love the Lord thy God with all thy heart, with all thy soul, and with all thy might") which includes teaching, remembering, and obeying the law.

At *Guide* 3.28, Maimonides argues that such love only becomes authentic through the acquisition of knowledge. It is therefore impossible to love God and remain intellectually complacent. If Judaism has any validity, the God we love is a God who stands for something, a God who Himself loves the widow, the orphan, and the stranger, a God who deplores ignorance and superstition, a God who will not allow people to make likenesses of Him. In Maimonides' view, one cannot love such a God without thinking deeply about what love means.

What can we know about this God? How can we talk about Him? What sort of conduct does He expect of us, and why? There is no choice but to ask these questions in a serious manner, and, having asked them, there is no hope of getting answers without the intellectual enterprise known as philosophy. Today, philosophy is a specialized subject taught at colleges and universities, but to understand Maimonides' devotion to it, we should not think of it as having so limited a scope. For him, philosophy is understood in the classical Greek sense of love of knowledge (philo + sophia), knowledge taken to its highest levels and subjected to the most rigorous standards, knowledge which includes all aspects of life.

Not that philosophy provides certain answers to every issue. We have already noted that Maimonides sometimes claims limited success for his own philosophic results. Even in passages where he argues that philosophic contemplation is the highest human good, he continues to make an important qualification: contemplation about things it is possible for a human being to contemplate. In a famous passage in *Guide* 3.51, Maimonides compares God to a ruler and worshippers to the people around Him. As with any ruler, varying degrees of intimacy are possible. Only those who observe the law *and* achieve mastery of philosophic demonstration can enter the inner court. Yet here, too, Maimonides reminds us of human limits.

> He ... who has achieved demonstration, to the extent that it is possible, of everything that may be demonstrated; and who has ascertained in divine matters, to the extent that it is possible, everything that may be ascertained; and who has come close to certainty in those matters in which one can only come close to it—has come to be with the ruler in the inner part of the habitation.

As we have seen throughout this study, Maimonides never forgets that we are fallible creatures.

Still, philosophy does provide a way of separating truth from error and of setting us on the right path. Without it, the educational message of the sacred books might be lost to us. Without it, worship might not lift us to the spiritual heights Maimonides describes. Without it, there would be little hope of resolving the perplexities in which we find ourselves. To the objection that such intellectual demands are difficult and burdensome, Maimonides would reply that certainly they are, but such difficulties and burdens were accepted the day the Jewish people undertook the responsibilities of being a light unto the nations. Unless the religion practiced by Jews can be presented to the nations of the world in an intellectually respectable way, its light may flicker and go out.

2. *Keeping the Light Alive*

For Maimonides, every ritual, prayer, or practice in Judaism is a means to the fulfillment of a single end: rejection of idolatry and worship of the true God. In a narrow sense, idolatry is the worship of strange gods or idols. But if we are to understand why the rejection of idolatry is so essential to Judaism — why idolatry is the sin of sins — we must recognize that it is not a simple phenomenon. Suppose a person were to ask why idolatry is objectionable. The harmful consequences of murder, stealing, and adultery are obvious, but what is so bad about bowing down to a piece of clay? Why have so many martyrs given their lives rather than submit to it?

In biblical times, idolatry involved a lot more than mere bowing to idols; it included serving them. Such service included human sacrifice, ritual prostitution, ceremonial mutilation of the human body, and countless other practices of torture and humiliation. Thus, the words of Deuteronomy 12:31: "every abomination to the Lord, which He hateth, have they done unto their gods." Such practices cause Moses to command and implore the people to blot out every sign of idolatrous worship and even the least inducement to it. In his discussion, Maimonides broadens the scope of the term *idolatry* (*Guide* 3.29–30), and to it adds such superstitions as wizardry, sorcery, the use of amulets, charms and incantations, and communications with the dead. On this issue, he is in perfect accord with the sentiment of Deuteronomy 18:10–11 and centuries of rabbinic commentary. But Maimonides goes still further in condemning astrology, the belief in demons and ghouls, rainmaking, faith-healing, fertility cults, and ascribing deity to animals — all abominations which he connects with an ancient people called the Sabians. Although his history may be open to question, his theology remains sound. Idolatry is not merely one or two immoral practices; it is a state of mind which brings out the worst in human behavior rather than the best. For Maimonides, idolatry is another name for ignorance, and as we have seen, ignorance is the prime source of evil. Maimonides condemns all such superstition as an insult to human intelligence and hateful to God.

To be sure, we must all contend with ignorance. Idolatry is threatening not only because it promotes ignorance, but because it worships ignorance; it asks us to look on ignorance with awe and respect, to see in ignorance a way of reaching or appeasing God. Idolatry amounts to the conviction that the deity is a force which can be placated, manipulated, or controlled by secret powers. It often depicts its god as unconcerned with or indifferent to reason and morality. Every page of *The Guide* attempts to show that Judaism was established to fight the temptation to idolatry in people's minds, and every commandment is framed with the same intention. To say that Judaism was established to fight the temptation to idolatry is to admit that idolatry does have an appeal. It is tempting to believe that wearing special clothes or charms, speaking certain words, or performing certain rituals can ward off sickness, death, poverty, and other misfortunes. It is tempting to believe that by calculating the positions of stars and planets, one can predict harvests or business cycles or the outcomes of personal relationships. It is tempting to believe that one can somehow coerce God into bestowing rain or good harvests, health or love, or other good fortune. For some, it is tempting to believe that divine favor can be courted by engaging in murder, mutilation, or other abominations. In every case, the appeal is clear: We are encouraged to believe that God must do *our* bidding rather than we do His. Idolatry cultivates the illusion that not God but *we* are in control of events, that any lust, greed, or hunger for power can be legitimated by indulging in some superstitious rite or practice.

To repeat: Idolatry stands opposed to rationality. In Maimonides' hands, rationality is not value-neutral; it sanctions conclusions opposite to idolatry. Human beings are *not* in control of the universe. According to *Guide* 3.13–14, they occupy only a small part of that universe, and it does not exist for their sake alone. They cannot at will turn cosmic forces on and off. They sometimes can heal the sick and improve their fortunes by educating themselves and appealing to rationally-arrived-at results, results available to all. In the last analysis, then, we must submit to the will of a greater Being than ourselves, a Being we can neither see nor depict in graven images.

In ancient times, the heart of idolatry lay in the worship of trees, animals, or figures made of clay, wood, or stone — all things we either make with our own hands or can destroy with our own hands. At *Guide* 1.36, Maimonides points out that no one ever thought these things were identical with gods; rather, they were images of gods that people could worship or pray to. But he goes on to say that there is a powerful tendency to focus on the image and forget the thing it depicts. If these images are supposed to possess magical powers, then idolatry construes god as a genie in a bottle. From such worship arises the illusion that we, not a superior Being, are in control. Maimonides credits Abraham with the discovery that God cannot be a body or a force residing in a body. As the creator of the universe, God is and must be separate from the universe: perfect, eternal, and radically one. The significance of this discovery is that God is not subject to our control, and by worshiping Him, we do not flatter ourselves but pay homage to a greater power.

In modern times, the lure of idolatry can still be felt. People continue to rely on good-luck charms, on astrological predictions, on fortune-telling and on secret cults; yet in our century, idolatry has taken forms Maimonides did not anticipate. Such idolatry attempts to deify a particular race or social and economic class. The founders of such idolatrous movements do not claim to be organizing religions, but insofar as they take race or class to be the ultimate truth, insofar as they accept no higher authority in the universe, insofar as they adopt superstition and reinstitute human sacrifice, they strongly resemble the idolatrous practices of old. Once more, they are convinced that human beings rather than God are in control of the universe; that and their contempt for rationality show that idolatry is by no means an occurrence unique to the ancient world. We have it with us still.

What all of these instances of idolatry have in common is that they treat something imperfect as if it were perfect. When Maimonides says that only God is a fit subject of worship, he means that only a perfect being can have unlimited claim on our attention. Throughout *The Guide*, he has been telling us what divine perfection implies: that God cannot be conceived in anthropomorphic terms; that God cannot be described in the usual subject/predicate way; that God is known not directly but through His consequences or effects; that God has a free and rational will; that the love of God is a rational process; that God's commandments are not arbitrary pronouncements, but a pathway to human perfection. No doubt worship of such a God puts enormous demands on the worshiper. One cannot participate in prayer or ritual blindly or uncritically. One cannot be content with pat answers to deep questions. One must subject one's conclusions to the most scrupulous criticism and be honest about what they do and do not prove.

We are now in a position to see why Maimonides thinks all the commandments lead to the rejection of idolatry and worship of the true God. To reject idolatry and everything it stands for, to commit oneself to the worship of a perfect being, one must do more than proclaim the existence of God. One must command a rational perspective on the entire universe. So it is be best not to think of Jewish law as a loose collection of practices and insights; rather it is a complete system, a worldview, which reaches its culmination in the first and second commandments. Fulfillment of the first and second commandments is thus a lifetime project. If Maimonides is right, they embody Judaism in its simplest and most intense form, a form which can best be understood as the kind of wisdom described in the eighth proverb: pure, straight, righteous, and more desirable than anything else in life.

3. *Where Is Maimonides Taking Us?*

The religion Maimonides envisions is, therefore, one in which enlightenment and spirituality go hand in hand, a religion in which everything is subject to critical scrutiny, in which everything must be explained and defended. The fact that something is written in Scripture carries great weight, for Maimonides never doubts that Scripture is the word of God; but what is written can never be the end of the matter. In the first place, Scripture can be interpreted in a variety of ways, and how to interpret Scripture can be decided only by rational argument. According to Maimonides, dogmatic appeals to literalism are of a piece with idolatry. They appeal to people who want to worship a visual image. In the second place, it is not enough to know that something is true; to reach a real understanding, we must ask *why* it is. At *Guide* 3.51, Maimonides asserts that those who can provide arguments on behalf of their opinions have achieved a higher level of worship than those who merely accept them on authority.

Can every worshiper achieve this sort of enlightenment? Can everyone appreciate the lessons of the Torah? Is it realistic to believe people will stop thinking of Judaism as another form of superstition, stop looking on sacred rituals as good-luck charms, and instead contemplate the glory of God in a pure, objective way, not asking God for favors but paying homage to His unique perfection? As the opening quotation from Ezekiel makes clear, Judaism has never been a slave to limited conceptions of what is "realistic." To many, it was unrealistic to think that the Israelites would reject idol worship and devote themselves to the service of a God they could not see. We can well imagine someone telling Moses as he came down from Mt. Sinai: Be realistic! And in view of the episode of the golden calf, such advice would not have been entirely out of place.

Still, Moses did come down from the mountain, and he expressed his outrage at what the people were doing, committing himself to the long, slow process of showing them the way to something better. However foolish people have been in the past, Judaism always holds out the hope that there is the possibility of acquiring a new heart and a new spirit. As long as such a possibility remains, simpleminded realism can never be allowed to carry the day. There must always be people who, like Maimonides, point the worshiper in a direction beyond anything he or she has known. As its best, worship should never leave us exactly as we are; it should make us different, change us, open us to higher levels of religious experience. In the last paragraph of *The Guide*, Maimonides quotes Isaiah 35:5: "Then the eyes of the blind shall be opened, And the ears of the deaf shall be unstopped." He takes these lines as a promise that, however difficult, the lessons of the Torah can and will be learned at some future time.

For the present, he recognizes that detailed philosophic argument is not for everyone. We have seen that *The Guide* is composed in the form of a letter addressed to an advanced student. What would Maimonides say to those who are just beginning? In a famous commentary on the Talmudic trac-tate Sanhedrin, he sets forth 13 principles that constitute the essence of Jewish belief. They are as follows: (1) the existence of God, (2) the unity of God, (3) the incorporeality of God, (4) the eternity of God, (5) that God alone is worthy of being worshipped, (6) the existence of prophecy, (7) that Moses is the greatest of the prophets, (8) that the Torah is of divine origin, (9) that the Torah is valid for all times, (10) that God knows everything we do, (11) that God rewards and punishes people for their actions, (12) the coming of the messiah, (13) eternal life.

This list is for beginners. It represents a minimal level of understanding, not a lifetime achievement. In writing such an abbreviated version of the system, Maimonides ran the risk that people would be content with short, pithy state-ments of belief and forget about the arguments on which they are based. It is not enough to say that God is one. We have followed arguments that show God is one in a unique way: He is not a normal subject of attributes and must be characterized more in terms of what He is *not* than of what He is. Along the same lines, it is not enough to affirm belief in prophecy. A number of theories purport to explain what prophecy is, just as a number of theories purport to explain divine providence, divine punishment or reward, and eternal life. In each instance, there are theories interpreting the phenomenon in a literal way and theories that see it as an allegory for intellectual fulfillment. Maimonides typically sides with the latter.

The fact that he does is evidence that the 13 principles were not intended to be the final word on Jewish belief. Like familiar passages from the Torah, they can be understood on a number of levels. The movement from elementary levels to more advanced should be viewed as more than accumulation of facts. As we move up the ladder, our outlook on the world becomes different. We begin to recognize that the universe is more vast than we may have thought, that God cannot be "above" the universe sitting on a throne, that prophecy does not have to be a miracle, that the messiah has better things to do than perform attention-gathering feats. In sum, Maimonides is taking us to a level of spirituality where stories and parables are replaced by eternal truths, where simple faith is replaced by reasoned argument, and where concern with the ebb and flow of personal fortune gives way to a broader perspective on life.

4. What Is More Important — Thinking or Doing?

A typical criticism of Maimonides is that he has put so much emphasis on intellectual comprehension that he has neglected, or encouraged his readers to neglect, the more mundane aspects of religious practice. Suppose it is true that prayer, ritual, dietary laws, and other day-to-day activities are means to an end: recognition of the eternal glory of God. Suppose, in addition, that someone were to achieve this end. If he or she has reached the level of spirituality Maimonides describes, what further need of the rituals designed to get them there? It is as if a person were to use a ladder to climb to the top of a building, and once on the roof, be persuaded to kick the ladder away.

Another way to look at this criticism is to consider the distinction between thinking and doing. To some people, it seems that Maimonides' view of spirituality is purely contemplative. Contemplation is the pinnacle of human perfection. If these people are right, it is hard to see why a person engaged in contemplation would want to interrupt it to take part in a ritual. The problem becomes more serious if we move from participation in rituals to acts of mercy or kindness. If contemplation is the highest human achievement, how then could a person be justified in leaving the study to administer to the needs of the sick, the poor, or the abused?

In the last chapter of *The Guide*, Maimonides addresses this criticism when he takes up the question of what the contemplation of God involves. He reminds us that no amount of contemplation will ever allow us to understand God as He is in Himself. All contemplation can reveal to us are God's effects, what were earlier referred to as *attributes of action*. Again Maimonides cites Exodus 33:13, where Moses implores God, "Show me Thy ways." Again he points out that what Moses apprehended were God's moral qualities: loving kindness, correctness of judgment, and righteousness. According to Maimonides, we know God in order that we may try to imitate Him. When it comes to recognition of the eternal glory of God, the distinction between thinking and doing breaks down. God is both an object of contemplation *and* a target at which to aim. To contemplate God, one must both recognize and aspire to a standard of moral perfection.

To the person who will not interrupt his contemplation to help the poor, Maimonides' reply would be that such contemplation is seriously flawed. It is not God the person is contemplating, because God is not morally indifferent. According to the Torah (Deuteronomy 10:18), He is deeply concerned with the plight of helpless or disadvantaged people. It perverts Maimonides' philosophy to argue that contemplation of God could lead to callousness toward the very groups He wants us to protect. Similar considerations apply to ritual. Insofar as ritual enhances the perfection of the soul and directs us to the commandments, it can never be dispensed with. At *Guide* 3.51, Maimonides emphasizes that even a person who has achieved the highest level of contemplation must still engage in worship. So virtuous action leads to contemplation of God, which, in turn, creates the conditions for more virtuous action, until at last virtue and knowledge become fused together.

5. Conclusion: Thou Shalt Teach . . .

We have come a long way in our consideration of Maimonides' philosophy, all of which is a reflection on the implications of monotheism, and thereby a discourse on the meaning of the *Shema*. In arriving at an overall assessment of his philosophy, we should keep in mind that, unlike some authors, Maimonides lets the reader know when his arguments are not as strong as he would like them to be. God is known to us through the attributes of action, moral qualities that emanate from God and seem to imply that He exercises a free, rational will. There are arguments to suggest that beyond the world we inhabit is the God who willed it all to be there. But Maimonides could not demonstrate this conclusion beyond a shadow of a doubt and said so. To his credit, it must also be said that the conception of a God who brought the world into existence by an act of will is part of an entire outlook on life. It is part of the view that God seeks the perfection of the human soul, has given us a body of law designed to help us achieve that perfection, and calls forth our highest moral and intellectual aspirations. Maimonides has shown how difficult it is to formulate a philosophically rigorous and authentic Judaism, but if he has not succeeded in every respect, he has proved to us how important it is to make the attempt. For, if the Torah is right in telling us, "Thou shalt teach these words to thy children . . . ," and if, after listening attentively, our children have searching questions about what they have been taught, we ought to be able to discuss concepts like monotheism, idolatry, prophecy, and commandment in a rational, coherent fashion. We ought to be able to tell our children, or anyone else who asks, why our prayers and rituals have meaning, why our love of God and His commandments binds us. If we cannot do so, if the words we are supposed to teach make no sense, if the rituals we practice are arbitrary, if the only explanation we can offer is "God's will," then we shall have failed in our obligations to our children, to ourselves, and to Judaism. And, of course, to Maimondes himself, for his rational view of Judaism is as lofty and moral a picture of the religion as has ever been written down.

CHAPTER SEVEN

MAIMONIDES OUR CONTEMPORARY

I call heaven and earth to witness against you this day, that I have set before thee life and death, the blessing and the curse; therefore choose life, that thou mayest live, thou and thy seed; to love the Lord thy God, to hearken to His voice, and to cleave unto Him; for that is thy life, and the length of thy days . . .

Deuteronomy 30:19–20

MAIMONIDES OUR CONTEMPORARY

1. A Steady Voice from a Troubled Time

The dominant theme which emerges from this study is that any conflict between faith and reason is less real than apparent; Judaism is justified by its claim to truth. Its symbols, ceremonies, dietary laws, and other rituals contribute to the educational mission to which the Jewish people have committed themselves: to further the understanding of monotheism and its implications.

When we think about Maimonides' philosophy, it is important not to form a false impression of his life. Maimonides did not inhabit a fairy-tale world in which people are immune to the daily struggle for survival and spend their time contemplating abstractions. After fleeing Spain, he spent much of his early adulthood fleeing across North Africa in the vain hope that he could find a community which would permit him to live in peace as a Jew. After arriving in Palestine, he witnessed the ravages of the Crusades and was forced to flee again. But even in the Jewish world, his life was anything but peaceful. His writings were controversial and often aroused resentment. He had firsthand experience of assimilation and religious zealotry. He therefore had ample opportunity to see that when true religion fails, the results are often violence, superstition, and death.

Clearly, Maimonides' age bears a number of similarities to ours. For him, as for us, Jewish survival could not be taken for granted. Forces outside the Jewish community sought to destroy it; forces inside sought to push it to extremes. Yet despite these forces, and despite a constant struggle against ignorance and disease, Maimonides never abandoned his commitment to rationality, he never maintained that philosophic inquiry is fruitless. When the Jewish community of Yemen faced extinction, he wrote his famous letter encouraging them to follow the precepts of the Torah, to understand that each precept contributes to the perfection of the soul, and to turn away from astrology, false prophets, and anything else that sins against reason. Reading this letter, a modern Jew cannot help but wonder what Maimonides would say if, by some miracle, he could write a similar letter to us. It is true, of course, that no one can speak on this issue with certainty. Once we remove an author from his or her age, we leave textual analysis and enter the realm of speculation. On the other hand, there is every reason to believe that were Maimonides to speak to us, he would stick to his principles and insist that we rededicate ourselves to the educational mission that defines Judaism and any religion properly described as monotheistic. To that rededication we now turn.

2. *Chosen for What?*

To understand Maimonides' predicament, we must recognize that throughout much of his life he fought a two-front war. On one front were those people who thought philosophy and science could answer all questions; on the other were those people who thought that everything we need to know is contained in the Torah. This does not mean that he opted for a simple fifty-percent compromise. Maimonides was convinced that every issue must be examined on its own terms, and every relevant piece of information brought to bear on it. Despite Maimonides' lifelong respect for Aristotle, he felt free to move in new directions when Aristotle's arguments lacked cogency. And despite his love for the Torah, he also argues (e.g., *Guide* 1.33–34) that only a person who has mastered such secular subjects as philosophy and science can decipher the wisdom the Torah contains. Maimonides is convinced there is no simple path to truth and therefore no simple path to religious enlightenment.

For Maimonides, Jewish education is first and foremost *education*. Rather than a process that erects barriers between Jews and other peoples, he wishes it to do the opposite: take truth from whichever source it originates and articulate it so that every person on earth can understand it. He rejects the idea that Jews should interpret the sacred books in a manner credible only to other Jews. Such procedure violates the plain sense of Deuteronomy 4:6 ("Surely this great nation is a wise and understanding people") and would be no more than a form of preaching to the converted.

Underlying Maimonides' view of education is a conviction that no deep-seated psychological differences exist between Jews and gentiles. All human beings are subject to the lure of idolatry, all are capable of grasping the truth, if it is put to them clearly and convincingly. It follows that all education worthy of the name must operate according to universal principles. In this respect, religion, like philosophy or science, seeks a truth that has nothing to do with blood or birth. If by *faith*, one means commitment to a belief for which there is no supporting evidence, then in Maimonides' conception of Judaism, there is little room for faith. One can, of course, have faith in the principles of the Torah; but the point of *The Guide* is that when it comes to these principles, evidence is available in abundance.

Unfortunately, centuries of persecution, mass death, and state-sponsored anti-Semitism have made it difficult for modern Jews to achieve so enlightened an attitude. Add to this that in the United States over the past twenty years there has been a noticeable increase in ethnic consciousness. Many people want to identify themselves as Afro-Americans, Asian-Americans, Greek-Americans, Mexican-Americans, or Native Americans. Each group is expected to wear its own clothes, sing its own songs, rediscover its roots, and make extravagant claims in its behalf. It is hardly surprising that many American Jews are puzzled when they read Maimonides. Instead of a plea for Jewish national identity, *The Guide* is a discussion of universal themes like negative theology, creation, and the limits of human knowledge. A frequent response to Maimonides' treatment of these ideas is: Why could a gentile not believe the same thing? To which Maimonides' answer would be: no reason at all. If monotheism has any validity, its appeal must transcend national boundaries. We have seen that Maimonides even allows for the possibility of gentile prophets.

The Guide is not the only writing where Maimonides deemphasizes the ethnic dimension of Judaism. When an ostracized convert asked whether he could use phrases like *"our* God" or "God of *our* fathers" when his ancestors were not Jewish, Maimonides wrote that Abraham's ancestry should be interpreted in a spiritual rather than a biological way. Abraham is the father of all those who adopt Judaism and profess the oneness of God. Unlike his contemporary, Judah Halevi, Maimonides does not argue that the Jewish people have a unique metaphysical status that they acquire at birth.

Maimonides believes Jewish identity must be preserved, and that many of the commandments are designed for exactly this purpose. But for him, Jewish identity is understood as participation in a spiritual community. That community is justified by the ideas to which it is committed, not the other way around. Customs, rituals, and ceremonies are worth preserving because they allow the community to propagate a defensible doctrine. Should Jews lose sight of that doctrine, the fact that they identify themselves as a people would count for little. The Edomites, Amorites, Moabites, Philistines, and other forgotten nations of the earth identified themselves as peoples, too.

Could another set of rituals, ceremonies, and customs allow a different people to propagate the same doctrine? The implication of Maimonides' position is that it could. If another set of laws stressed the unity and incorporeality of God, creation, freedom, social harmony, moderation of the passions, and respect for strangers, widows, and orphans, Maimonides would have to take it seriously, no matter what the origin of the people proposing it. This does not mean he would reject Jewish law, but he would have to deem the other laws morally legitimate in their own right.

In our day, Maimonides' position is often ignored. We put so much stress on the concept of peoplehood that it is hard not to conclude that ethnic considerations come before philosophic ones. The dangers of making ethnicity para-

mount are: (1) People will become so enamored of the ceremonies, rituals, and folklore that they will neglect the intellectual growth which is supposed to follow and forget about
the idea of monotheism; and (2) In the cases where intellectual
growth does follow, it will overlook the universality of Judaism and focus on its cultural or religious peculiarities.

Maimonides' opponents often parrot the objection that
he is an elitist, maintaining that the number of people who
can achieve a complete understanding of monotheism and
enter the inner court of God is limited. Ethnic identity, on the
other hand, has one undeniable virtue: Everyone can participate in it. It does not take years of study or intense concen-
tration to feel one is part of an ethnic group. The question
Maimonides forces us to ask is whether such participation is
enough to sustain Judaism. Will it satisfy the spiritual longings of the people and enable them to love God in the highest
way? Will it lift them to the heights achieved by Jewish
communities in Babylonia, Egypt, Spain, France, and Ger-
many? In an age when traditional values are under attack,
when religious fanaticism sweeps whole countries like a
plague, does Judaism provide the intellectual wherewithal to
tackle difficult problems, to rediscover eternal truths, or does
it habitually fall back on the concept of chosen people, never
explaining what this people is chosen *for*?

These questions are too broad to be answered in a yes-
or-no fashion, but they raise issues that need to be confronted. Although education often begins with a mythical or
rudimentary account of a subject, eventually it must move to
a reasoned, careful study. We would not expect a college
student to explain the American Civil War by citing popular
legends about Abraham Lincoln or to describe the operations
of the federal government by repeating campaign oratory.
We would point out that it is impossible to learn the lessons
of history or to grasp the meaning of current events unless
one adopts a critical attitude and pays attention to detail. Yet
suppose that when asked about the implications of monotheism, a college student referred to legendary accounts of Moses.
Or suppose the student still thought of God as a bearded man
sitting on a throne. Would we object, or would we claim that
in religion, the critical attitude appropriate to subjects like

American history or political science must give way to faith? Would we accept lower standards for Jewish education than we would for secular, arguing that the primary function of Jewish education is to make people *feel* Jewish? If the answer is yes, if we are afraid that reasoned argument is not necessary or might turn people away from Judaism, then, in Maimonides' view, we have done the religion a disservice by closing off the educational process before it has a chance to work. In so doing, we have robbed Judaism of the primary goal it seeks to accomplish.

To the objection that only a few people can understand the religion at the level Maimonides seeks, the reply would be that the same is true of a subject like the Civil War. Only a few individuals can grasp the totality of so complicated an event. But this does not prevent us from teaching American history as rigorously as possible, structuring each class according to the students' level of comprehension. It is true, as Maimonides points out at *Guide* 1.34, that approaching a subject at too early an age can lead to confusion, but putting a subject off indefinitely and relying on pat answers can have the same effect.

Even at advanced levels, though, Jewish education is often inward-looking. To appreciate the richness and subtlety of *The Guide*, one would have to study Maimonides' three most important predecessors: Plato, Aristotle, and Al-Farabi. To understand *The Guide's* subsequent influence, one would have to study those on whom Maimonides had a noticeable impact: Aquinas, Spinoza, Leibniz, and Kant. To some people, these authors are tainted. Plato and Aristotle were pagans; Al-Farabi was a Muslim; Spinoza was an excommunicated Jew; Aquinas, Leibniz, and Kant were Christians. Should one read these authors in order to obtain a *Jewish* education? Should Jewish culture be understood in light of developments in other cultures?

The easy answer is that the proper study of Jews is other Jews. The superficial plausibility of this answer explains why many Jews regard *The Guide* as strange and unappealing. The author they want to study is the Maimonides of the *Mishneh Torah*, the Talmudic expositor, not the philosopher. The problem is that Maimonides himself claimed to be both.

At *Guide* 2.11, he points out that some Jews regard the philosophic opinions of gentiles as alien to Judaism. This was as true in the twelfth century, when a number of Jewish authorities tried to ban *The Guide*, as it is today. To the degree that Jews isolate themselves from broad trends in Western philosophy, they isolate themselves from Maimonides, and, in Maimonides' judgment, from the wisdom contained in their own sacred books. We have seen that when read in a literal or unsophisticated way, many passages in the sacred books are no better than Greek mythology.

3. Finding Access to God

If Maimonides fought a two-front war on education, he also fought one on obedience to law. Here, too, the conflict concerns spiritual shortcuts. Like group identity, the commandments are a means to an end: They create the atmosphere in which one can pursue the rational love of God. Many people object to the idea that spirituality requires intellectual exertion; to them, Judaism ought to provide easier access to God than Maimonides allows. These sentiments can be found in both orthodox and liberal circles.

Orthodoxy stresses continuity with the past and the need to preserve the totality of Jewish law. Since he believes the Torah is of divine origin, Maimonides supports both sentiments. But he would deny that simple obedience is the be-all and end-all of Jewish aspiration. At *Guide* 3.51, he warns against allowing worship to become a perfunctory duty in which one never reflects on the meaning or purpose of what one is doing. At 3.52, he reiterates that one cannot love God in ignorance even if one obeys the commandments and prohibitions. So it is not enough to keep the Sabbath, observe the holidays, obey the dietary restrictions *if* one believes one's religious duties end there. These activities are obligatory but should not loom so large in a person's mind that there is no room for reflection and study. Judaism requires discipline, not exaggerated piety.

This does not mean he wants to abandon fasting, praying, and other rituals; on the contrary, he is convinced they are an integral part of religious life. What he wants to do is insure that they achieve the purpose for which they were intended. If they become simple exercises pointing to nothing beyond themselves, they would lose much of their value. Separating milk from meat will not improve one's health, or insure one's happiness, or earn one a place in heaven unless it is part of a transcendent framework, a framework in need of constant articulation and refinement.

On the surface, a person obsessed with ritual may seem to take a demanding approach to religion; but ritual, too, can be a shortcut, a mechanical way of courting favor with God. For some people, it is easier to participate in highly regimented activities than to engage in reflection and study, easier to cook milk and meat in separate pots than to consider alternative accounts of creation. If a person lacks the aptitude for philosophy, Maimonides sees nothing wrong in obeying the commandments and living a traditional Jewish life; the problem arises when we look on such a person as an ideal, suggesting that nothing further needs to be attempted.

In one respect, liberal Judaism is the mirror image of orthodoxy. Liberals do not consider obedience to law the last word in religion. They agree with Maimonides' contention that people must be weaned away from idolatry in stages, so that it is appropriate to inquire into the historical context in which ritual occurs. And they agree that "God's will" is not sufficient explanation for why a ritual ought to be observed. As we have noted, Maimonides did not intend to change the law, but to justify it; nevertheless, other generations sometimes overlook an author's intentions. Maimonides is frequently invoked by people who believe that Jewish law must continually adapt to the circumstances in which it finds itself.

In another respect, liberal Jews join hands with the orthodox in attacking Maimonides for being too intellectualistic. While orthodox Jews stress the importance of tradition, liberals often want a religion that is more "experiential." Experiential religion can take several forms: political activity, community service, feelings of love or personal satisfaction, mystical awareness. In all cases, there is an attempt to move away from philosophic reflection and to recapture what Martin Buber called "actual lived concreteness." According to this view, God is not an abstract principle but a living presence or personality who must be confronted by individual worshippers intent on preserving their individuality. As Buber argues, each of us must approach God "in the singleness of his being and the singleness of his life."

Maimonides would be sympathetic to the claim that religion must have an experiential component. He organized a medical clinic, treated patients, became a polemicist for important causes, so it would be wrong to interpret his rationalism as an attempt to escape from reality. What separates Maimonides and the advocates of experiential religion is that for him, religious activity is not a purely personal matter. Comforting the sick and caring for the less fortunate are sacred obligations. Just as we must take certain steps to insure the health of our bodies, Maimonides thinks that we must take steps to insure the health and welfare of our souls. While we have to allow for physical and spiritual differences among individuals, these differences are not as great as the advocates of experiential religion would like us to believe. The perfection of one soul is similar to the perfection of another. Both culminate in love of the same God. It is misleading, therefore, to say that each person must approach God in the singleness of his or her being. If we truly understood the singleness of our being, we would recognize that individual differences are overshadowed by shared duties and common aspirations. In Maimonides' judgment, these duties and aspirations form the substance of Jewish law, which is why he thinks a traditional understanding of the law should be kept intact.

To repeat, it would be wrong to suppose that Maimonides is opting for a middle-of-the-road position between orthodoxy and liberalism. There are aspects of both he would applaud. What would disturb him is the extent to which each distrusts reason and attempts to replace it with something else, because for Maimonides there are no credible substitutes. Reason is not just another human faculty; we have seen that according to *Guide* 1.1, it is the very image of the divine in us. When reason is no longer the focal point, when people decide that personal differences or outward shows of piety are more important, the Judaism that results is badly warped. Although such a religion may promote the survival of a people, it would not promote better understanding of monotheism, and without such understanding, even survival would become problematic. All the sanctuaries, monuments, or bar and bat mitzvah celebrations could not hide the fact that the Jewish people no longer had a sense of purpose.

4. Why Trust Reason?

If large segments of the Jewish community have come to distrust reason and look for substitutes, they are hardly alone. Ours is an age in which reason is under attack from many quarters. At the most rudimentary level, this attack takes a familiar form: Not everyone is as rational as Maimonides seems to think. In stressing the importance of reason, he has overlooked the extent to which human behavior is influenced by love, hate, greed, jealousy, national pride, and other emotions. To this objection there is a simple reply: Considering the period in which he lived, and the turmoil he endured, Maimonides could not have been so naïve as to believe that everyone is rational. He insists that rationality is an ideal to which God calls us but to which we need not necessarily respond.

The attack on rationality can be reformulated at a higher level. Some people protest that rationality is unduly restrictive. To argue that all human perfection culminates in love of the same God is to suggest that everyone must seek perfection in lockstep fashion. Others maintain that we are so conditioned by our environment that it is either foolish or inauthentic to suppose we can grasp the eternal truths Maimonides discusses in *The Guide*. What we call *reason* is so much a part of cultural or historical factors that it is no more then a set of self-serving prejudices. When people say they are appealing to reason, they are in fact appealing to the interests of a particular class or group. Wealthy communities find rationality in laws that favor the wealthy, poor communities in laws that favor the poor. Still others insist that in a world in which violence and terrorism are commonplace, reason is a luxury we can ill afford.

To these people Maimonides' philosophy cannot help but seem archaic. If Freud is right and human beings are motivated chiefly by aggressive and antisocial impulses, if Marx is right and economic necessity is the single most important factor in determining historical change, if Nietzsche is right and human beings' highest aspiration is the will to power, how could anyone living in the twentieth century take Maimonides seriously? Has his conception of reason not been thoroughly debunked? In the sense that few thinkers, Jewish or gentile, continue to look on reason as a form of salvation, the answer is yes. So if the question is about prevailing attitudes, one would have to conclude that the debunkers are right.

But why should the question be interpreted this way? If it is true that the twentieth century has come to distrust reason, it is *also* true that the twentieth century has been one of the most brutal and bloodthirsty ever. Two world wars have been fought, genocide and mass murder have been integral parts of state policy, racial and tribal warfare have taken an increasing toll in human life, and even in places where political order is relatively secure, there is a widespread conviction that nothing is sacred. In the United States, violent crime, infant mortality, industrial pollution, and economic dislocation have become facts of life. In many instances, what passes for reason is not an image of the divine but a grotesque caricature: bureaucratic planning that destroys whole neighborhoods in the name of "urban renewal"; economic thinking that encourages market manipulators and quick-buck takeover artists; military thinking that used body counts or kill ratios to devise strategy in Vietnam.

Maimonides would analyze this litany of woe to see if it is a series of unrelated events or a record of what we may expect when reason is no longer held in high regard. Once reason is forsworn, once we abandon hope of resolving our conflicts or expressing our convictions in a rational manner, do we free ourselves from a useless burden or leave ourselves no other choice but settling our conflicts by brute force? Once we abandon rationality, we sever any tie we might have to the divine. It is then no accident that in our century human life has been cheapened, and God seems to have hidden His face. If human beings are merely power-hungry animals unable to rise above the biases and interests of their own culture, is there any reason to hope that the abominations and savageries of the twentieth century will not repeat themselves?

If Maimonides' assessment of the human condition is accurate, the answer is no. In his view, it is not God who abandoned us, but we who have turned our backs on Him. The problem is that we cannot approach God unless we make the effort to rise above the cultural and economic circumstances in which we live, make the effort to see the world from a higher, broader perspective. If monotheism is valid, then all people and all existing things have a common origin in God. If this premise is denied, then we are determined by cultural and economic imperatives alone. Forever trapped in our own partial, particular worldview, why bother to learn about others'? Why not simply assert *our* claims, insist on *our* rights, ignoring or opposing all others'?

Maimonides is part of a long line of thinkers who maintain that reason is an instrument for human betterment, a way of looking at people not in terms of what they are but what they might become. For Maimonides, reason involves a commitment to a way of life which shuns complacency, dogmatism, and inflated estimates of one's own needs and accomplishments. Whatever access we have to God is through a lifelong devotion to such a commitment and its ideals.

Maimonides would be the first to admit that the life he recommends is fraught with risk. The path of learning contains pitfalls, and it is true, as many of his opponents insist, that what *passes* for reason is often only another set of prejudices. But if the life of reason does pose risks, it nonetheless remains our best hope for improving our lot. Distrusting reason may avoid risk, but it mandates the certainty of failure, especially if such distrust of reason implies confidence in the barrel of a gun, in brute force, in solving our problems, in resolving our conflicts. Unfortunately, the testaments to such failures litter the landscape of our time.

5. Still a Compelling Book?

In examining Maimonides' heritage to us, we have gone beyond the jot and tittle of his text to discuss its wider implications. To ask whether *The Guide* is still compelling is to ask whether it is worth talking about today. Can we read it as if it were addressed not to a particular student in the twelfth century but to the people of every age?

If the answer to that question is yes, then we have conceded a great deal to Maimonides. In effect, we have agreed that monotheism is neither a simple idea nor a transitory one. Although saying the *Shema* twice a day puts one in a community of Jews espousing monotheism, it does not make clear what that community is committed to. The intellectual accomplishments of a community can decline or decay. More than one nation has lulled itself to sleep by mindlessly repeating a cherished bit of dogma or performing a comforting ritual. If asked to summarize Maimonides' achievement while standing on one foot, the proper reply would have to be that explaining, understanding, and defending monotheism is the highest human calling. This and this alone offers us the possibility of cleaving to God.

The Guide is written in the spirit of Deuteronomy 30:19, a passage Maimonides frequently cites. The choice between understanding and intellectual complacency has been set before us. Properly interpreted, it is tantamount to a choice between life and death. Maimonides' advice to our age, and to every age, is to choose life. If Maimonides is right, understanding monotheism is not something the Jewish people just happen to do; it is their very lifeblood. With it, they are a community in covenant with God; without it, they are merely another of the many peoples who insist that their way of life is somehow superior to all others. If the former has been enough to sustain the community through centuries of historical turmoil and strife, the latter is not.

SUGGESTIONS FOR FURTHER STUDY

SUGGESTIONS FOR FURTHER STUDY

The secondary literature on *The Guide* is vast and extremely demanding. The following suggestions for further reading are made with two purposes in mind: (1) These readings can be understood by people with no technical training in philosophy; and (2) They are likely to be available in a decently stocked library or bookstore.

1. Maimonides' Life

For a fascinating intellectual biography of Maimonides, see:

Abraham Joshua Heschel, *Maimonides*, translated by S. Heschel (1935; rpt. New York: Farrar, Straus, Giroux, 1982).

This book represents an early work by an author who himself became one of the leading Jewish theologians of his time.

For a translation and commentary on some of Maimonides' most important letters, see:

Crisis and Leadership: Epistles of Maimonides, translated and edited by A. Halkin and D. Hartman (Philadelphia: Jewish Publication Society, 1985).

This volume should dispel any notion that Maimonides was an ivory-tower intellectual.

2. English Translations of The Guide

The two most readily available translations are:

The Guide for the Perplexed, translated by M. Friedlander, second edition (1904; rpt. New York, Dover Publication, 1956).

The Guide of the Perplexed, translated by S. Pines (Chicago: University of Chicago Press, 1956).

The Pines translation is now the standard by which all others are measured.

3. Maimonides Anthologies

For selections from *The Guide*, as well as helpful notes and commentary, see:

RAMBAM, Readings in the Philosophy of Moses Maimonides, edited and translated by Lenn E. Goodman (Los Angeles: Gee Tee Bee, 1985).

For people interested in reading selections from the entire corpus of Maimonides' writing, the best anthology is:

A Maimonides Reader, edited by Isadore Twersky (New York: Behrman House, 1972).

4. Reading The Guide

A number of different approaches have been taken to reading *The Guide*. For one very different from that pursued in this study, see the works of Leo Strauss in:

Leo Strauss, *Persecution and the Art of Writing* (Glencoe, Illinois: The Free Press, 1952).

Leo Strauss, "How to Begin to Study *The Guide of the Perplexed*," in the Pines edition of *The Guide*.

Strauss puts heavy emphasis on the Talmudic prohibition against teaching creation and other esoteric matters in public. He therefore concludes that *The Guide* is an esoteric book whose real message is given in hints or clues. The approach taken in this study assumes *The Guide* is a traditional work of philosophy in the dialectical mode. The issue is whether the dialectical mode is a deliberate attempt to be evasive or an attempt to begin with simple ideas and work toward more complex ones.

For an approach more compatible with the one taken here, see:

Joseph A. Buijs, "The Philosophical Character of Maimonides' *Guide* — A Critique of Strauss' Interpretation," *Judaism* 27 (1978), 448–457.

5. Maimonides' Philosophy of Religion

Three well-done studies are:

Isadore Twersky, *Introduction to the Code of Maimonides (Mishneh Torah)* (New Haven: Yale University Press, 1980).

David Hartman, *Maimonides: Torah and Philosophic Quest* (Philadelphia: Jewish Publication Society, 1976).

Yeshaiahu Leibowitz, *the Faith of Maimonides*, translated by J. Glucker (New York: Adama Books, 1987).

But notice how different Hartman's picture of Maimonides is from Leibowitz's.

A new volume that will be a welcome contribution to the literature is:

Menachem Kellner, *Maimonides on Judaism and the Jewish People* (Albany; SUNY Press, forthcoming).

6. The History of Philosophy up to Maimonides

The best multi-volume study of the development of Western philosophy is that of Frederick Copelston. With respect to Maimonides, the two most relevant parts of the series are:

Frederick Copelston, *A History of Western Philosophy, Volume I: Greece and Rome* and *Volume II: Medieval Philosophy, Augustine to Scotus* (Westminster, Maryland: The Newman Press, 1965).

Much of medieval philosophy is Aristotelian in character. For a good introduction to Aristotle, see:

G.E.R. Lloyd, *Aristotle: The Growth and Structure of His Thought* (Cambridge: Cambridge University Press,1968).

The best available anthology of medieval philosophy is:

Philosophy in the Middle Ages, edited by Arthur Hyman and James J. Walsh (Indianapolis: Hackett Publishing Co., 1973).

7. Jewish Medieval Philosophy

The best-known secondary source in this area is:

I. Husik, *A History of Medieval Jewish Philosophy* (1916; rpt., New York, Harper & Row, 1966).

Also see the relevant chapters in:

Julius Guttmann, *Philosophies of Judaism*, translated by D.W.Silverman (New York: Schocken Books, 1973).

For an anthology of Jewish medieval philosophy see:

With Perfect Faith: The Foundations of Jewish Belief, edited by J. David Bleich (New York: KTAV, 1983).

Notice that this book is organized around Maimonides' thirteen principles.

8. Negative Theology

A very helpful article is:

Schubert Spero, "Is the God of Maimonides Truly Unknowable?" *Judaism* 22 (1973), 66–78.

9. Advanced Treatments of Maimonides or Jewish Rationalism

For those with some background in philosophy, the following books or articles are recommended:

Maimonides: A Collection of Critical Essays, edited by Joseph A. Buijs (Notre Dame: University of Notre Dame Press, 1988).

Marvin Fox, *Interpreting Maimonides* (Chicago: University of Chicago Press, 1990).

Daniel H. Frank, "The End of the Guide: Maimonides on the Best Life for Man," *Judaism* 34 (1985), 485–495.

Lenn E. Goodman, *Monotheism* (Totowa, N.J.: Littlefield, Adams & Co., 1981).

David Hartman, *A Living Covenant* (New York: Macmillan, 1985).

Menachem Kellner, *Dogma in Medieval Jewish Thought* (Oxford: Oxford University Press, 1986).

David Novak, *The Image of the Non-Jew in Judaism* (Toronto: Edwin Mellon Press, 1983).

Creation and the End of Days, edited by D. Novak and N. Samuelson (Lanham, Md.: University Press of America, 1986).

Maimonides and Philosophy, edited by S. Pines and Y. Yovel (The Hague: Martinus Nijhoff, 1986).

Studies in Jewish Philosophy, edited by N. Samuelson (Lanham, Md.: University Press of America, 1987).

Steven S. Schwarzschild, *The Pursuit of the Ideal*, edited by Menachem M. Kellner (Albany: SUNY Press, 1989).

Kenneth Seeskin, *Jewish Philosophy in a Secular Age* (Albany: SUNY Press, 1990).

Schubert Spero, *Morality, Halakha and the Jewish Tradition* (New York: KTAV Publishing Co., 1983).

Harry A. Wolfson, *Studies in the History of Philosophy and Religion*, Vol. 1 & 2, edited by I. Twersky and G. H. Williams (Cambridge: Harvard University Press, 1973–77).

The greatest Jewish rationalist of the last hundred years is surely Hermann Cohen. For an anthology of Cohen's writings, see:

Hermann Cohen, *Reason and Hope*, translated by Eva Jospe (New York: W. W. Norton, 1971).

10. Christian Scholasticism

A superb exposition of Christian rationalism is:

Joseph Owens, *An Elementary Christian Metaphysics* (Milwaukee: The Bruce Publishing Co., 1963).

Do not be misled by the word "elementary" in the title. The book is very challenging. Notice, however, how much this study is concerned with metaphysics (what is) rather than ethics (what ought to be done).

INDEX